PARTNERSHIP
in Urban Education:
An ALTERNATIVE School

PARTNERSHIP
in Urban Education:
An ALTERNATIVE School

AASE ERIKSEN
and
JOSEPH GANTZ

PENDELL
PUBLISHING
COMPANY

International Standard Book Number: 0-87812-054-8

Library of Congress Catalog Card Number: 73-89103

CONTENTS

ACKNOWLEDGMENTS

We would like to acknowledge all those involved in the implementation process: students, teachers, parents, community members, university and board of education personnel, and all others who gave of their time and energy to make the West Philadelphia Community Free School a reality. This book could not have been written without the efforts of a great many people.

In addition, the following people were indispensable in preparing this book from the manuscript stage to final publication: Fred Fiske, Rosemary Hennessey, and Jane Tierney.

Thanks beyond words to Judith Messina, colleague and friend, who stayed with us throughout the long process of preparing the manuscript for publication.

INTRODUCTION

In the last ten years, existing educational programs and facilities in our large urban areas have grown scandalously obsolete. Many of the big high schools are overcrowded and badly equipped. Students spend four years trying to fit themselves into a rigid system in which they are unable to meet informally with teachers or to pursue their own interests. There is no time for spontaneous study, no room for individual initiative. As a result, many students have given up trying to learn or never ever begin trying. Instead, their concern is with "getting by," "passing the test," graduating.

The solution to this pressing social problem cannot be found in abstract theory or in isolated pockets of experimentation. Instead, the problem must be faced head-on; the existing urban school structure must be dealt with on its own terms, and on a scale which will effectively ease the present crisis. One way of alleviating this crisis in education is by giving all members of society a choice in the kind of education they want for their children. One means of providing such a choice is by offering alternatives within the public system.

This book focuses on the process of implementing one such alternative school within a public urban system. The pedagogical model presented herein and the problems encountered in molding it from its conceptual beginnings to the realities and frustrations of a living school define and illustrate the implementation process. To identify and illustrate the problems inherent in organizing and operating an alternative school we have used the West Philadelphia Community Free School as a case study. We have not tried to evaluate the Community Free School, but rather, have offered observations and analysis on two different levels: 1) harnessing the resources of an urban community to sustain the existence of an alternative school, and 2) the alternative school itself as providing an innovative approach to learning. Within these two levels several important aspects of the implementation process are dealt with:

1) Parents and members of the community became active participants in determining the goals of an educational facility which directly affected their own and their children's lives;

2) The partners to this experiment demonstrated to varying degrees a willingness to share in the overall responsibility of educating urban youth;

3) The alternative school itself, physically small and scaled to human size, attempted to create a total learning environment;

4) Finally, in spite of all the problems, delays, and frustrations in implementation, this alternative school did, in fact, become a reality.

The book is arranged to illustrate as clearly as possible the implementation process: 1) a description of the goals and objectives of the PASS Model (Public Alternative School System) and an outline of its specific components; and 2) a description of the three phases of the implementation process. It is likely that anyone — parents, teachers, school administrators, and/or students — who is interested not only in developing alternative educational environments and models but also in implementing them will have to grapple with problems and questions similar to those described here. Hopefully, this book can alert parents and educators to these issues and perhaps make the going easier for future alternatives.

CHAPTER I

THEORY: THE PASS MODEL

THEORY: THE PASS MODEL

The PASS Model (Public Alternative School System) is designed to give parents and students a choice in public education. PASS schools represent an alternative coexisting with traditional public high schools within a metropolitan or suburban school system and offering new educational goals and methods. The diversity which such schools can provide may act as a stimulus to the public system as a whole and can serve to strengthen rather than weaken it.

The major goals, outlined below, illustrate the philosophy of this alternative form of public education:

1.   Humanize education.

    A.   Provide a learning environment in which students believe and feel that they can control what happens to them.

    B.   Provide a learning environment in which students feel they have a real part in the development and success of their school.

    C.   Provide a learning environment in which students feel that what they think, feel, say and do can make a difference.

    D.   Provide an atmosphere of security, affection, and trust without fear of recrimination for "failure."

2.   Develop within students a sense of freedom which includes being both free and able to make decisions.

    A.   The development of self-pride.

    B.   The development of the ability to make choices and take risks.

3.   Develop within students a feeling of responsibility for the success of others.

4.   Promote mastery of basic skills.

5.   Widen students' horizons and raise their levels of aspiration.

GOAL ACHIEVEMENT

The achievement of these goals encompasses three concepts: structure, educational program, and environment.

Structure

The PASS school is a cooperative effort among four partners: the community, the board of education, institutions of higher learning, and local business and industry, all of whom share the responsibility for the education of the children and adults of their community. A community board comprised of representatives of all four partners, including students, parents, and teachers, is responsible for the implementation and development of the school and for the supervision of its daily operation. Indeed, the active and ongoing involvement of the partners in the implementation and development process is essential if the school is to meet the needs of the community which it serves.

These community members may participate through acts of service and decision-making involving the alternative school as well as

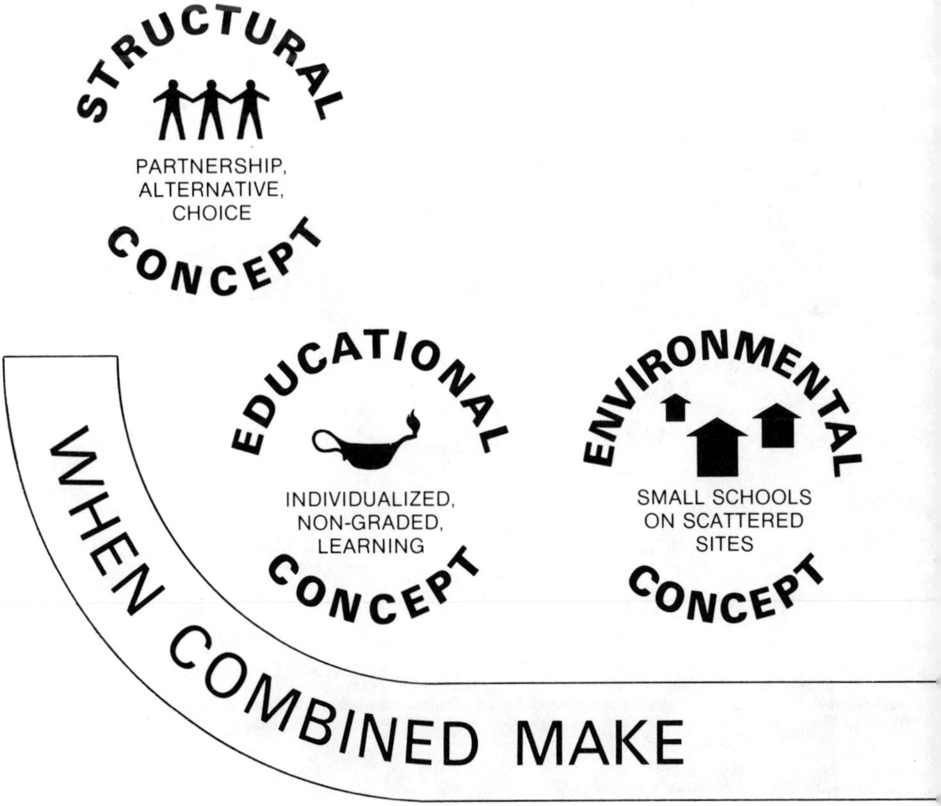

STRUCTURAL

PARTNERSHIP,
ALTERNATIVE,
CHOICE

CONCEPT

EDUCATIONAL

INDIVIDUALIZED,
NON-GRADED,
LEARNING

CONCEPT

ENVIRONMENTAL

SMALL SCHOOLS
ON SCATTERED
SITES

CONCEPT

WHEN COMBINED MAKE

through freely participating in the teaching-learning processes themselves. They represent the vast pool of resource material and expertise present in every community. By offering their services and knowledge, community members not only alleviate the economic burden of paying for the sharing of such expertise, but also turn the resources of the community inward toward its own improvement and for the ultimate benefit of all partners.

The PASS school is part of the public school system and thus, the board of education is a member of the partnership. The alternative school is tied into the system directly at the superintendent's level and is under the superintendent's jurisdiction.

However, an affiliation may also be established between the PASS school and an already existing public school which can serve as a resource center. This larger "mother-school" may provide special facilities such as a gymnasium, large rooms, typing facilities, and a library. The student body of the mother-school would be the pool from which PASS students would be selected. Besides functioning as a resource center, the mother-school can also still provide a traditional education program for those who want it.

The institutions of higher learning also provide facilities to supplement those of the PASS school when necessary: gymnasium, theater, laboratories, and playing fields. Students, faculty and other members of the university community are encouraged to take part in the educational and extracurricular programs, contributing their time, services, and talents to high school students of the community. The benefits to the university are several, including a laboratory for training teachers, a research ground for university faculty and a means whereby undergraduates may be of service to the community and also gain course credit by doing so.

A business advisory board should be organized with leading businessmen, and the chairman should become a member of the community board. This business advisory board will help to involve as many community business and industries as possible in the planning and development of outside or community enrichment programs enabling students to explore business opportunities in an atmosphere free from the pressures of hiring, firing, and professional training.

The business community, in turn, has the advantage of meeting potential employees informally and on a personal basis. The immediate results are often beneficial to both groups, and the future implications are central to the continued economic and social well-being of the community. Business also benefits through continued relations with the community, university and school system and by being constantly aware of current community thought and opinion, as well as by having a forum for expressing its own ideas.

The physical structure of the PASS school is based on a house system which may be adapted to fit the needs of any metropolitan environment. The school consists of houses placed according to a scattered site plan which distributes them within the community.* The houses, containing no more than 200 students each, operate independently, each comprising a school in itself. The school board provides funds for the maintenance of the buildings and the students contribute by helping to paint and decorate their houses. As the student population grows, additional commercial or residential buildings will be acquired and renovated, a process which greatly reduces the need for expenditure of capital funds in the building of new schools.

Development of a personal supportive atmosphere within the houses is focused in the family group, a key in the structure of the house system along with the small student body. This unit consists of one teacher to approximately 12 to 15 students. It is within this cohesive unit that students and teachers plan academic and other activities which all family group members can enjoy and participate in. It is here, too, that students can feel free to discuss any problems they may encounter as well as issues of concern to the school community. The family group relationships among teachers and students are the starting point for all other relationships in the house, for they provide a stable and secure element within a flexible and ever changing program.

In addition to the family group units, students within each house may organize a steering committee which in addition to students may include one or two teachers for the purpose of organizing the student input into the program and for dealing with matters of day-to-day operation of the school. Students may also establish a judicial board

---

*See Aase Eriksen, (Philadelphia, 1971), a study of the scattered site plan conducted with a grant (No. 71-7063071) from the Department of Health, Education and Welfare.

including one or two teachers for the purpose of dealing with disciplinary problems within their house unit. The leadership within the house unit is supplied by the head teacher, who does not occupy a bureaucratic position, but rather accepts the responsibility for leadership in his house. In addition to teaching, the head teacher delegates responsibilities to others in the house and sees to it that administrative tasks which are shared by the teachers are carried out. He is responsible for ensuring that the educational model is adhered to and acts as a "contact" person for parents and the community board.

Since each house is viewed as the students' school, parents also become directly involved with the educational program through an active parent group. This group makes available to the students and teachers the wide variety of services which parents can offer.

Educational Program

The educational program of the PASS school has two major parts: the inside program and the outside program. The first part of the program deals with the basic curriculum studied in the houses; the second part is carried on in the community. Throughout both aspects of the program the work is nongraded, eliminating the grades traditionally known as nine, ten, eleven and twelve, and providing for individual instruction and heterogeneous groupings of students. There may be variations within each house, however, in subsequent implementations of the PASS Model.

Inside Program

The major concern of the inside program is the development of basic skills in class work, small group work, and individual conferences. The program consists both of givens and choices. That is, each student must study courses in the humanities, in math and in science each year. In addition, he has a choice of other courses to supplement the required studies.

Humanities: One of the foundations of the humanities program is the reading and writing workshop. Each student is scheduled into the workshop for two or three periods a week. He may also choose other courses within the humanities program, some of which are interdisciplinary. Some may be minicourses scheduled for four or six weeks. Students may choose several minicourses during a single semester.

Mathematics: The math program is carried on primarily in a workshop structure so that the work is individualized. In this way, several levels can be taught at the same time in the same room. Since math is required of all students, group work using math games is often set up to help students who are either uninterested or at a low level of understanding in math. Math could also be taught by means of a computer terminal as well as through traditional academic courses for those students who wish to pursue them.

Science: Although science is required of all students, it should be kept in mind that all students are not aspiring scientists. Therefore, the school focuses its science program on an integrative approach. A major part of the program centers around such areas as ecology and urban environment. Having contact with a college or university provides teachers and students with help for advanced pursuits as well as with lab facilities and equipment.

Foreign Language: Foreign languages are offered for students who wish to study them, particularly those who intend to go on to college.

Along with these studies, interdisciplinary courses are designed to give students the opportunity to learn how the various disciplines are dependent upon one another and the extent to which they touch on the students' own lives. This approach also gives teachers the opportunity to work together and to strengthen their understanding of other disciplines.

Throughout the in-house program, emphasis is placed on team work. Teams consist of teachers or of teachers and students who assist them. These students have hours scheduled into their rosters and receive course credit for this work. Emphasis is thus placed on encouraging students to help teach other students.

Outside Program

The outside program brings the student into direct contact with the "real world." Courses are established on location in businesses, industries, and institutions in the community. Students take at least one of these outside courses each semester. They work in hospitals and offices, learn to run computers, handle business transactions and pursue interests in the arts and academic disciplines.

By entering the doors of business and industry, students travel in both a physical and social sense. They begin to raise the level of their aspirations once they are shown the wide range of opportunities open to them. When they see for themselves what it takes to achieve new goals, they gain a new perspective on basic academic skills: after all, math becomes a whole new subject when you're handling a bank account or programming a computer. The outside program increases the students' areas of experience and competence, encourages them to make choices and take risks further afield, and give them real reasons for mastering basic skills. In addition, the program should be viewed as supporting students' special interests as well as furthering advanced students in certain subjects.

Equally important is the fact that having students in the outside program reduces the student-teacher ratio within the house, thus permitting small group work and individualized instruction to take place.

The structure of the overall program provides for each student to design his individual roster, selecting courses from both programs. Travel time to outside courses is built into the rosters along with some free time to give students periods in the week, other than lunch hour, during which they may do whatever they like. No courses are scheduled to meet every day in the week for two reasons: 1) to provide for the flexibility needed to offer a variety of courses, and 2) to provide breaks in the weekly schedule giving students some days in the week without their required or least favored courses.

In keeping with the educational goals of the PASS Model and with the structure of courses offered, students are evaluated on an individual basis. That is, they receive no grades for their work, but rather receive from each of their teachers a detailed written evaluation of their progress twice each semester. If necessary, these evaluations may be translated into letter or number grades for college entrance applications.

Environment

The PASS school is based on the concept of humanized education, offering high school students the opportunity for individual growth through a program that is flexible enough to bend to their specific needs and concerns. The humanistic objectives are inherent not only in the structure and pedagogy of the school program but also in its environment. Both the social and physical dimensions of the school environment suggest the educational philosophy on which the school is based and both have a direct bearing on its success.

As stated above, the PASS school should provide a social and educational atmosphere in which students believe they can control what happens to them and in which students have a sense of security, affection, and trust. Working under these conditions, teachers can help students acquire a sense of freedom and the self-confidence to make choices and take risks. The overall environment should be one in which students and teachers feel relaxed and where their relationships become a more natural process. As a result of such mutual interaction and support, and in the absence of fierce competition and recriminations for failure, students can develop a feeling of responsibility for the success of others.

The physical environment of the school has a great influence on the learning process. Space, color, and arrangement will suggest to the student the kind of learning environment envisioned by the planners; it tells how learning shall take place and how one should view the schools.*

A community school such as the PASS school opens the school environment to the whole community, inviting all of the members of that community to have a part in the learning process. For some this means teaching, for others it means learning, for still others it means both. In order to realize the goals of humanized education in a supportive social atmosphere, the physical environment of the PASS school must provide the setting to invite such action.

The traditional high school building offers the students little opportunity to impose a personal touch on their surroundings. Because of its size and design the traditional school is not conducive to humanized team relationships and flexible learning situations. In addition, there are no open areas for relaxed, casual interaction among the students. The physical layout of the PASS school offers solutions to these problems.

---

*See Aase Eriksen, *Scattered Schools* (Philadelphia, 1971)

The individual house should be small. The building must be close to human scale — an area of space not too large for everyone to know and feel free to move around. The limited size, moreover, will make it possible for students to play an active part in decorating and caring for the building.

The space, color, and arrangement of each house must create a workable and personal concern, yet be functional for the activities planned. The interior design should provide for a variety of work areas.

Scattering schools throughout the community makes them more accessible to the members of the community and provides a more natural way to use other institutions. Adults of the community will also find it more inviting to come into the smaller neighborhood school, either to help as paraprofessionals or to participate in sessions for themselves. The scattered site plan is singularly important for the development of alternative schools within a public system. It provides not only alternative goals and methods, but accommodates a growing student population at a low relative cost to the board of education. This frees funds for other needed expenditures in the way of equipment, materials and personnel, thus strengthening the public system as a whole.

CHAPTER II

IMPLEMENTATION PROCESS

IMPLEMENTATION PROCESS

The process of transforming the PASS Model into the West Philadelphia Community Free School was long and complex. Because the project was without precedent, because the innovative school was to operate within the jurisdiction of the public school system, and because of the broad spectrum of individuals and groups involved, the implementation process took more than a year. The Community Free School was implemented in three phases: During Phase I (August, 1969 — February, 1970), support for the school was solicited, negotiations among the partners were carried on, and plans for the program were developed; Phase II (February — June, 1970) was the first semester of the school's operation; in Phase III (June — December, 1970), the program was expanded and refined.

By recounting in some detail the events and processes involved in the implementation of the West Philadelphia Community Free School, we hope to offer assistance to others concerned with developing alternative schools in other metropolitan areas. The success of the Community Free School depended first upon the participation and cooperation of the representatives of the residential community, the university, the board of education, the business community, the teachers and the students. The story of the implementation process thus begins with a description of each group's contribution.

THE PARTNERSHIP

All members of the community share the responsibility for the education of the children in their community. Each of the four "partners" involved in the implementation of the Community Free School had definite and distinct contributions to make in the formulation and realization of this alternative project. During the implementation process, partners assumed particular responsibilities consonant with their areas of influence, expertise and experience.

Responsibilities within Partnership

The Residential Community: An operating community action group first initiated negotiations with the University of Pennsylvania and the Board of Education of Philadelphia and thus provided the momentum for the development of the Community Free School. This community group assumed two primary responsibilities: first, its members worked on a continuing basis with the other partners, expressing the needs and concerns of community parents, students, and residents, and participating in every phase of the program's development. Secondly, the community members, some of whom were also parents of school-age children, continued to work within the community itself, familiarizing parents and students with the new program, calming fears and relieving apprehensions when necessary, and urging community residents to take an active part in the program's development.

The University: Throughout the implementation process, the University of Pennsylvania provided extensive support for the Community Free School project. University personnel were released from academic or administrative responsibilities, in order to apply their professional expertise to the implementation of the Community Free School. University faculty, students, and administrators contributed to the educational program, offering learning opportunities both inside and outside the school buildings.

The support of a prestigious university was an invaluable asset: the leverage which members of the university applied was just what the community members needed in negotiations with the school system. In addition, the university provided short-term assistance, such as funds and facilities, when delays or unforeseen circumstances arose.

The university was thus crucial in providing for a smooth implementation process; without the flexible, substantial assistance and involvement of the University, the Community Free School would never have become a reality.

The Board of Education: The primary responsibility of the Philadelphia Board of Education to the Community Free School was to provide facilities, equipment, and personnel for the school's day-to-day operation. The school board allocated the same per pupil allotment to the Community Free School as to regular metropolitan high schools. This meant that the same ratio of certified teachers to students was guaranteed for the Community Free School as to every other city school. In addition, the school board agreed to differentiated staffing classifications at the Community Free School. This allowed paraprofessionals to assume teaching responsibilities in the new school.

In addition to providing an operating budget for the Community Free School, the school board was also expected to provide support for the school, drawing on the resources and administrative expertise of the school system. In particular, special facilities in the mother-school such as auditoriums and athletic fields were to be made available for use by students from both schools.

The Business Community: The principal focus of involvement by the business community was the outside program. Community businessmen worked with university and community participants in developing the outside program; they designed courses within their own institutions and released employees to help plan and teach these courses. In addition, community businessmen helped involve other members of the business community in the Community Free School project, explaining the purpose of the school and encouraging them to participate actively in the outside program.

Benefits within Partnership

The Residential Community: The structure, size and program of the PASS model make it possible for members of the community to be actively involved in the education of their children. It gives them the opportunity to help implement schools which meet the needs of their children.

Interrelationship of Needs

The structure also gives members of the community a chance to work with different groups in the community such as businesses and institutions.

The Board of Education: The PASS model provides the school system with a model that can function as one alternative within that system. As this model functions in the form of Community Free Schools, it opens up new ways for the community to become more directly involved in the educational process. The success and problems found in the implementation of this model can provide new ideas, new curriculum, etc., for the existing school system. It can also be viewed as a laboratory for in-service teacher training, in which regularly appointed teachers spend a semester in a Community Free School and then return to their previous positions with new ideas, methods and concepts.

The University: The model provides a structure for a meaningful way in which the university as a whole can render a contribution to the community of which it is a part. Benefits accruing to the university are that the PASS model:

1. can provide a laboratory for teacher training, management and administrative training, and the training of educational factors, that

2. the implementation of such a model creates new research topics and problems for several disciplines, that it

3. gives university faculty a chance to teach high school students and provides a basis for a better dialogue between university/college professors and high school teachers, and that it

4. provides field experience and feedback for professors who would be interested in writing and developing material meaningful to public education.

The Business Community: The model provides for active involvement of community business and industry in the Community Free School. The outside program enables students to explore business opportunities, and employers meet potential employees and get to know them on a personal basis. The short-term results are often beneficial to both groups, and the long-range implications are central to the continued economic and social health of the community.

Additionally, members of the business advisory board are given the opportunity to relate on a continuing basis with community representatives, members of the school system and the university community. Through the community board, community businessmen remain abreast of the diverse currents of community thought and opinion, and in turn have a forum for expressing their own ideas.

PHASE I: PLANNING

Initiation of Project

In the spring of 1969, a group of West Philadelphia community residents visited the University of Pennsylvania. In discussions with University officials, the community residents described the inadequate school conditions in their community: too many students and not enough space in the classrooms. In 1969, teachers in West Philadelphia High School were attempting to teach 4300 students in facilities for 2400. Needless to say, they were not meeting their goals. Students cut class or failed to come altogether; incidents of vandalism were high, as was the rate of suspension; that a large number of students had lost interest in school was evidenced by low test scores and a high dropout rate; also a good percentage of those who did graduate from high school still lacked the basic skills training necessary to compete for a place in college or in the job market.

In response to the request for help from the community group, whose leader was Mrs. Novella Williams, University President Gaylord Harnwell and Provost David Goddard asked one of the authors to consult with the community group. She held extensive meetings with community residents to determine the specific needs and desires of West Philadelphia parents and students. The educational model which resulted from these discussions called for the establishment of community-based, community-directed public schools located on sites scattered throughout the community. The model proposed to reawaken student interest in school through a small, personalized school

24

environment and through an innovative educational program. The model also included a structure for sustained involvement of community and university representatives, as well as representatives from the board of education and the business community. The model thus provided the means whereby the resources of the community could be turned inward for the improvement of the community's public schools and for the benefit of all members of the community.

The bulk of planning and coordination of the West Philadelphia Community Free School project was carried out by those involved in the initial discussions at the University of Pennsylvania. In August, 1969, the West Philadelphia Community Advisory Board was formed. This community board consisted of community residents, headed by Mrs. Novella Williams and Reverend William Barrett; Francis Betts, III, the University President's Assistant for External Affairs; Walter Scott, principal of West Philadelphia High School; and the authors. Board meetings were scheduled at semimonthly intervals, but usually met even more frequently during the implementation process.

Initial Support

From August, 1969, to February, 1970, representatives of the four partners worked to build a foundation of support for the school. Within the University, interest in the project was high. President Harnwell and Provost Goddard participated actively, by helping to organize and by addressing several luncheons held in support of the project. These meetings proved instrumental in bringing members of the business community into the program.

Philadelphia School Superintendent Dr. Mark Shedd also supported the project from the beginning. His interest and concern, and the assistance of members of his staff helped to bridge the gulf between the community school project and the giant bureaucracy of the school system. The District Superintendent, Dr. Marechal-Neil Young, also worked closely with West Philadelphia High School principal, Walter Scott, to make a place for the Community Free School within the public school system.

During the planning phase, members of the community board were active in the West Philadelphia community, publicizing the concept and soliciting support for the school. They attended meetings at West Philadelphia High School and telephoned parents and students to explain the concept and structure of the Community Free School and to encourage its acceptance into the community. They held meetings with district administrators to iron out specific problems and attended luncheons along with the authors to help describe the program and elicit the support of community businesses and other institutions.

By attending the luncheons sponsored by the University, members of the business community learned about the project. They responded with interest, though some were hesitant. In the follow-up meetings, ways were explored in which individual businessmen might contribute or become involved in the Community Free School. Many institutions ultimately committed themselves to participate in the outside program and began to work with the school planners to develop that aspect of the Community Free School.

Acquiring and Renovating Facilities

The University of Pennsylvania was instrumental in assisting in negotiations with the Philadelphia Board of Education for acquiring and preparing school facilities. By September, 1969, a site for the school had been selected, approved by the school board, and acquired. The last remaining hurdle, and one which led to agonizing delays and several postponements of the school's opening, was the approval of the facility by the city zoning board. Largely on the basis of the school board's failure to adequately explain the concept of the West Philadelphia Community Free School, the zoning board withheld its approval. Though the major renovations had been completed, the zoning board still considered the site "inadequate." In addition, the Licensing and Inspection Office had not yet approved the site, principally on the grounds that a fire escape still had to be installed. While estimates went out and preliminary work began, another site had to be found.*

---

*As it turned out, it was October of the next year before the original facility was approved, on the basis of a carefully prepared presentation by the community board, with support from students, University representatives, and members of the business community.

An alternative site on University property was found and was loaned to the Community Free School. While renovations were still underway, pressure from all sides to open the school had grown so intense that it was decided to start the first semester on February 1, 1970, regardless of what facilities were available at that time. As a result, the Community Free School did open its doors on February 1 but in four separate, hastily assembled locations.

Selection and Training of Teachers

Professional Teachers: The first stage of the selection procedure consisted of a written application submitted to the selection committee (three community board members, the principal, and the educational consultant).** This application included a resume, two recommendations from students who had worked with the applicant in previous classes, and a statement as to why the applicant wanted to teach in the Community Free School. Essay questions, such as the following example, were an important part of the application.

> Suppose all of the syllabi and curricula and textbooks in the schools disappeared. Suppose all of the standardized tests — city-wide, state-wide, and national — were lost. In other words, suppose that the most common material impeding innovation in the schools simply did not exist. Then suppose that you decided to turn this "catastrophe" into an opportunity to increase the relevance of the schools. What would you do?

Once the applications were received, teacher applicants were interviewed individually by the selection committee. The interview consisted of from three to five questions which determined whether the applicant met the selection critieria of the model. The interview board was looking for answers on a general scale that fit the selection criteria and for more specific answers that fit the teacher description contained in the PASS Model.

**When the school expanded after the first semester, a new committee was formed to select teachers for the three houses. This committee included, in addition to members of the community board and the authors, teachers and students who had worked in the Community Free School during the first semester.

The teacher's training prepares him to deal in depth in at least one field and in a cross-disciplinary manner with other fields. He has concern, not only for the student, but also for the community and its long range needs and interests. This he recognizes and deals with in the teaching-learning process. The teacher possesses personal strength, self-confidence, warmth and understanding in relating to and dealing with people.

Teaching Criteria:

1. Openness to and flexibility for change on many levels.

2. Ability to teach without a textbook.

3. Ability to create workable new teaching strategies as they are called for and to allow for students to create their own.

4. Ability to deal with a student centered situation . . . so as to encourage learning experiences which the student discovers and acquires for himself.

5. Ability to create a curriculum and learning situation that is experience-based and which, therefore, demands the ability to discard plans and create new ones as they are called for.

6. The teacher should realize the importance of possessing listening and clarification skills, i.e., listening to the student and helping him clarify what he wishes to express.

7. Ability to deal with students on a one-to-one basis, allowing for diversity within a class and programs geared to each student's needs, interests, and abilities.

8. Ability to work with other teachers, staff, and students in teaching and developing new curricula; ability to critique other teachers and openness to share the feedback from students and colleagues.

9. Primary concern for the process of learning rather than for the subject matter goals; ability to view learning from the learner's perspective.

10. Respect for students and community members as persons with feelings, attitudes, and experiences which command attention.

Personal Qualities:

1. A teacher should know his discipline in terms of its major principles and concepts and their practical application.

2. Training and/or experience in a field other than one's discipline; it may be related to that discipline or entirely unrelated to traditional disciplines.

3. Sufficient background and experience to view and apply the learning-teaching situation through an inter-disciplinary approach.

4. Evidence of interest and involvement in community affairs, particularly community education.

5. Evidence of interest and involvement in a variety of areas, e.g., travel, music, politics, art, community affairs, etc.

6. Personal strength and self-confidence.

7. Insight into oneself; the applicant should know why he is a teacher.

8. Warmth and concern for people.

9. Ability to relate to students and other teachers in a team approach to learning.

By October, 1969, a staff of eight certified teachers had been selected for the Community Free School, all of whom had taught at West Philadelphia High School, six as regularly appointed teachers and two as Harvard University teaching interns. It had originally been planned, for financial reasons, that the entire certified staff be drawn from teachers already working within the school system. However, the reluctance of system teachers to apply for positions necessitated the hiring of new teachers.

Community Teachers: While certified teachers were being interviewed and selected, community teachers were also being solicited. These teachers were required to be members of the community in which the school was located. They were asked to submit a written application to the community board and to appear for an interview at one of the board meetings. Criteria for the selection of these teachers were designated by the community board in consultation with members of the professional staff.

It was determined that the role of the community teachers should be four-fold. First, they were to work with students and teachers to create a meaningful learning experience by 1) concentrating on individualized instruction — especially skill development; 2) teaching in an area in which the community teacher had special training or experience: i.e., music, mechanics, sewing; 3) assisting in reading and writing workshops and in recreation projects. Second, the community teachers were to help in the socialization process of the Community Free School to help students understand the concept of the Community Free School and the direction of the educational process. Third, they were to assist the smooth and efficient operation of the Free School, both administratively and educationally, by helping with students, moving students to their proper activities, making physical improvements, and working with teachers to evaluate and improve the existing curriculum. Finally, the community teachers were to help present the Community Free School to parents and members of the immediate business community. They, as well as the certified teachers, were to act as community liaisons.

Outside Teachers: The active participation of university faculty and student teachers in the inside and outside programs was also sought.

In the fall, the provost wrote a letter to university faculty and students, urging them to become involved as instructors in the outside program. Several faculty members and students responded and proceeded to develop outside courses in their areas of interest and competence. In addition, many undergraduate students offered to teach in the school as volunteer student teachers, assisting the certified teachers in gathering resource material and helping out in other ways.

Perhaps the most significant involvement of the academic community in the school came in the cooperation with the experimental intern program in the Graduate School of Education. Seven graduate students from this program became full-time intern teachers at the Community Free School.

By October 15, a complete teaching staff for the Community Free School had been selected. The teachers represented an extremely heterogeneous group: some had little teaching experience, others had little familiarity with the local community and its needs and some had experience from very traditional teaching environments. It was, therefore, decided to set up a series of training sessions, inviting all teachers to attend. Because the certified teachers could not be released from their classrooms at West Philadelphia High School until the Community Free School opened, the training sessions were scheduled after school, in the evenings and on weekends. To avoid union problems, teachers volunteered to come to these sessions.

The purpose of the training sessions was to familiarize teachers with the new learning environment, to help them get to know each other, to orient them to the needs and values of the local community, and to encourage them to develop new approaches to teaching and curriculum. Several sensitivity training sessions were run by a professional group of teacher trainers. Activities during these meetings included role-playing games, meetings with community members, writing projects, informal discussions, and evaluations of activities. Teachers attended informal dinners sponsored by the university. During the first week of December, the university also made available to the Community Free School its "retreat" outside the city. Teachers and staff, along with community members and students, spent two days on this quiet estate, participating in relaxed discussions and curriculum planning meetings.

The community teachers took part in the teacher training workshop held for the certified teachers (see Staff Development, pp. 52-57). In retrospect, the community teachers acknowledged that perhaps additional separate training session would have been worthwhile as it was often assumed that they knew more about teaching than they actually did.

Selection of Students

In order to assure the heterogeneous grouping of students, the community board decided that the student body of the Community

Free School should be selected according to the following criteria: 1) 50% to be randomly selected from the student rolls of West Philadelphia High School; 2) 50% to be selected from a list of applicants from West Philadelphia High School; 3) the Community Free School should have the same percentage of students in each grade level as the mother school. For the first house, however, only the first and third criteria were adhered to.

A letter of invitation was sent to each student selected. The students were to decide in consultation with their parents whether or not to attend the new school and parents were to return permission slips indicating their acceptance or rejection of the offer of admission. Community board members telephoned parents in order to answer any questions which they had and finally sent letters to those who were to attend, telling them which house they were to be a part of and where to report. Of the students whose names were drawn, all but 37 decided to attend the Community Free School.

Selection of Staff

Besides selecting teachers and students, the community board was also responsible for appointing all staff positions: an Educational Consultant/Director of the project; Assistant Director/Administrative Assistant; a Community Coordinator* to direct the outside program; and a head teacher, one of the certified teachers, who would assist teachers with organizational and administrative matters and act as a liaison between teachers, staff members, and the community board.

Development of the Inside Program

In addition to meeting after school and on weekends for the training sessions, teachers also participated in intensive planning sessions and discussions to develop the initial educational program for the Community Free School.

---

*See appendix for role description.

During these meetings, which ran from mid-October until the school opened in February, many alternative curriculum proposals, teaching procedures and techniques, and organizational structures were considered.

Plans were initially set to open the school in December; in October and November, teachers were, therefore, working under a deadline to develop an interdisciplinary curriculum and establish administrative procedures for running the inside educational program. When the opening date was postponed due to a delay in obtaining adequate facilities, this pressure was somewhat relieved, and more thorough planning was possible.

During the first weeks of school, students would spend all day in family groups. The curriculum would be structured around an interdisciplinary theme, "The Individual in the Urban Environment." A large box would be filled with objects drawn from the environment. These objects would serve as visual stimuli to the students who would select an object and proceed to explore, with the assistance of teachers from different disciplines, its relationship to the environment.

Plans for the first week of school were worked out in detail ahead of time. These included organizational and administrative procedures, such as selecting family groups, obtaining equipment, setting up a student steering committee, and establishing standards for attendance and evaluation. In addition, a series of concrete activities were designed to encourage students and teachers to get to know each other during the all day family group meetings and to begin working on the interdisciplinary unit. The structure of these activities was carefully worked out, while the particular sequence and implementation of the activities were left up to the individual family group teacher. In this way teachers would be able to draw on predesigned activities and, at the same time maintain a great deal of flexibility in the classroom. Teachers were assisted throughout the planning stage by undergraduates from the university, who helped assemble and organize curriculum materials for the first week of school, as well as for the remainder of the interdisciplinary unit.

Funding and Trade-offs

The Community Free School is a public school. Its teachers are drawn from the public school system. Its facilities are owned and operated by the Philadelphia Board of Education, and its materials and books are supplied by this institution. In general, its program conforms to the basic requirements set by local and state authorities.

As a public school its financial maintenance comes under the responsibility and control of the board of education, or whatever public body, i.e., city council, controls public school funds and allocations. Large public school systems have elaborate and complex disbursement systems which permit little if any flexibility for the allocation and/or reallocation of funds. Moreover, because of the size of the system and the cumbersome procedures used for administering it, it is equally difficult to convince responsible administrators of the need and/or validity of transferring monies from one area to another.

At the same time, it is obvious that, if it is to become a reality and be incorporated into the regular system, an alternative school must not require great additional expense. It is possible to operate schools in this model with little or no additional cost through a system of trade-offs within and between systems and institutions.

The trade-off concept suggests that the cost of services not required by the Community Free School be transferred to finance the operations which are unique to this alternative program. For example, the traditional high school employs "counselors" to advise students and deal with student problems. In the Community Free School, the family group teacher fills, to a large extent, the role of counselor to the students in his family group. The cost of hiring and maintaining a traditional counseling staff is thus unnecessary and the funds allotted in the mother-school for this purpose might be reallocated to the budget of the community coordinator's office in the Community Free School.

Another trade-off is to pay community teachers with funds presently designated for nonteaching assistant positions in the mother-school. The small size of the Community Free School house unit makes these nonteaching assistants, who are essentially peace-keepers and guards, unnecessary.

A large area of saving would be in the area of capital expenditures. Locating and renovating already existing facilities is a great deal less costly than building new facilities for a growing student population. The cost of the new University City High School building which was recently completed in West Philadelphia to house approximately 2500 students and appropriate staff was a multimillion dollar proposition. However, the cost of locating and renovating 12 Community Free School units to house approximately the same number of students and staff would be considerably lower.

The entire question of trade-offs is a very sensitive area particularly in public bureaucracies. It is implicit in this concept that a local community board in conjunction with members of the central board of education can reallocate and disburse public funds. Indeed, this has been the crux of the dilemma in most experiments with urban decentralization of educational authority. It is clear that the settlement of this delicate and highly political question would take many months in any given alternative program. Yet, because of the innovative structure of many alternative programs, initial additional funds over and above teachers' salaries and the regular per-pupil allotment for materials, supplies, and current operating expenses, are required. This kind of additional funding is needed in the following areas:

1. Personnel not covered by traditional high school or board of education categories, e.g., community teachers, community coordinator, facilitator.

2. Innovative materials, books, and curricula. Most public school systems have access to a great variety of such materials, but because of the procedures involved in acquiring them for any one teacher or class, they must be ordered many months before — a real difficulty for an alternative school which seeks to meet the often rapidly changing needs and interests of students.

3. Research and evaluation: to conduct ongoing teacher training, process evaluation of the implementation of the educational program, and the development of new research techniques and methodology. It is an unfortunate, but well documented, fact that alternative schools are forced constantly to "justify their existence" by proving that they are

doing the job they have set out to do *better* than anyone thought possible. Because of this kind of pressure it is essential that sound techniques and appropriate research and evaluation be built in to an alternative school model at its inception.

We believe that within a reasonable time period — perhaps three years — the operation of the Community Free School, or a similar alternative, should and could be funded almost exclusively by the public school system within its regular operating budget.

PHASE II: THE FIRST SEMESTER

The first weeks of any experimental school project are bound to be chaotic and disorganized, even when plans have been carefully laid and are successfully carried out. In the case of the Community Free School, the initial reaction of the 200 students from traditional West Philadelphia High School to the new environment was one of bewilderment ánd consternation. Although introductory meetings between students and teachers and parents had gone well, and although the first weeks of the educational program had been planned in some detail, few staff members had predicted the extent of student disorientation. The abrupt dislocation from the traditional system left the students without guidelines or directions to follow. The most immediate student response was disbelief; the most daring students showed this in their questions. One teacher described the first day of school:

The students couldn't conceive of an informal school. All they could do was react as though they were still at West Philadelphia High School. Most of their questions were about grades and structure, rather than about the ideas of the new school.

The first months of the school program, then, were spent in setting up the inside and outside programs, encouraging students and staff to develop working relationships among themselves, and orienting them to their new educational environment.

The Programs

Inside Program: The nongraded curriculum of the Community Free School was designed to correspond to the guidelines and requirements established by the Pennsylvania Department of Education. It was deemed important, however, that, before the various subject courses began, students and teachers should have the opportunity to work together in a very flexible educational environment which would combine study, informal discussions and meetings, and concrete activities relating to the new environment. For the first month, therefore, the inside educational program was organized around the interdisciplinary theme, "The Individual in the Urban Environment." While the intent was to provide students and teachers with as much freedom and flexibility as possible, it was recognized that students also needed a "fixed point" of continuity in an environment which presented them with so many abrupt changes. A decision was made to set up family groups on the first day of school. Each teacher would be assigned a group of 12 to 15 students, and they would begin working on concrete activities together. The family groups would meet all day every day during these initial weeks and would serve as the nuclei for relationships among students and teachers in the house as well as a starting point for involvement in the educational program.

During the first hectic weeks of school, the family group proved to be a principal factor in the survival of the program. The continuity of the family group was instrumental in helping students through a period of transition. Family group activities, focused on the interdisciplinary theme, were the only real program structure during these first weeks. While each family group developed differently, reflecting the uniqueness of the students and teacher involved, all family groups built some degree of cohesiveness and interdependence; this closeness lasted throughout the school year. And, as students grew more familiar with one another, they began to reach outside the family group in the same way.

The family group teacher was the student's guide, counselor, friend, and teacher during the first few weeks. When the students had a problem, the family group teacher would be his defender, his advocate, his facilitator. Several teachers remarked that through the family group they were able to get to know each student personally and that this was the most positive and constructive result of the first weeks of school.

37

As the term progressed, students grew more confident, and the importance of the family group diminished in relation to the educational program. However, the family groups remained intact, and students met with their family group teachers at irregular intervals throughout the first semester to receive and discuss evaluations, plan specific activities, and to deal with administrative matters or emergencies.

One specific family group activity which began as soon as the house opened was the decoration and renovation of the school building. The building was an old storefront, with three floors, plenty of light, sufficient classroom space, several large open areas, and offices for the school staff. House decoration was both a necessary and beneficial educational activity. Not only did the old building need livening up, decorating activities also provided another "fixed point" in the educational program, with nearly unlimited creative potential and tangible, visible results for students to see. By working on the building, students began to feel it was their building; in effect, they were permitted to express themselves not only in their relations to teachers and to one another, but also in the visual terms of their environment.

Naturally there were limits to the amount of work students could do on the building. The basic renovation and construction work was completed before school opened (in accordance with zoning requirements), and furniture was provided. Students and family group teachers concentrated on painting and decorating the walls, keeping the building clean, and making minor repairs and alternations. Looking after the building became a communal activity which encouraged students to work together and enabled them to join teachers in a common effort. Several students who would perhaps have made a smaller contribution to the school in a traditional classroom or in extra-curricular activities were able to make a meaningful contribution by helping with design and decoration.

There is no question that the appearance of the school building affected those who worked and studied within. When the building is neglected, it demoralizes students and teachers alike. An exerted effort to restore and adorn the building can be a rejuvenating device for the educational program. Concern for the environment was a continuing process in the Community Free School and was a learning experience for students as well. Students were always free to change the environment when they wanted; each change reflected the desires and abilities of the individuals in the house. Clearly, the small school building was a valuable asset to its inhabitants, a unique environment, flexible and adaptable to the ideas and impulses of the school community.

Besides decorating and maintaining their own school environment, students and teachers were also introduced to new and flexible uses of space within the building. Students had some difficulty adjusting from the traditional use of space to the open environment of the Community Free School. First, it was emphasized that learning could take place anywhere in the building — not in an "English cubicle" to the left and a "math cubicle" to the right, but rather in a variety of locations — in small rooms or open spaces, inside or outside the building; in addition, the learning experience did not end with a bell on the hour, but would often continue through free time periods or lunch breaks, in staff offices and hallways.

Secondly, students were encouraged to be mobile. In a traditional urban high school, the size of the building and of the student body calls for administrative procedures and rules, such as rigid class schedules and hall passes, which limit movement. In addition, in urban schools gang members "cordon off" certain areas of the large school buildings, and students moving through these areas run the risk of attack or reprisal from fellow students. In the small school environment of the Community Free School, students were encouraged to move around the building freely, in and out of staff offices, in the classrooms and open spaces. No boundaries between strictly "academic," "staff," and "open" areas were set up, and students began to feel that they could walk anywhere without fear of reprimand or reprisal.

Students had never before experienced this freedom to move about within a school building unhindered. One consequence of this new policy was a burst of student exuberance and a drastic rise in the noise level. Clearly, the traditional concept that learning takes place only in a quiet and orderly environment had been discarded. Since this rise in noise and movement levels had been anticipated, carpets, acoustical tile, cork boards and other furnishings had been supplied and installed throughout the building.

Moreover, the open environment of the Community Free School permitted and encouraged students and teachers to be comfortable as they worked, sitting on the floor if they liked. Thus, carpets were necessary.

Thirdly, it was recognized that in order to fully appreciate the open environment, students needed both free access to "public space" and a certain amount of "private space" which was their own property and responsibility. Therefore, space was set aside for individual student lockers, which they could use throughout the year as personal storage space. Later in the semester, students representatives took the initiative in securing space on the third floor of the building, for the exclusive use of students for recreation, informal gatherings, and student-initiated activities.

One other aspect of the inside program should be mentioned in closing: the Scholastic Aptitude Test coaching program which was set during the first semester in conjunction with the Educational Testing Service in Princeton, N.J. In accordance with the model goal of "raising students' levels of aspiration," the implementors were determined to provide those students who wanted post-high school education with the skills needed to pass the SAT and qualify for college admission. Therefore, a deliberate test-coaching course for students who planned to go to college was designed, and others who were not sure were encouraged to participate. While the test-coaching program was more fully developed during the following year, the groundwork for its implementation was laid during the first weeks of school, and the first test-coaching program was offered during the first semester.

Outside Program: Because of the interdisciplinary program and the all-day family group meetings, the outside program began several weeks after the Community Free School opened. First, students were given a catalogue listing and describing more than 50 outside courses which had been set up in community businesses and other institutions. A sample of course offerings: "An Introduction to Computing" offered at the University City Science Center; "Laboratory: What's It All About?" at the Children's Hospital of Philadelphia; "Neighborhood Planning" at the Young Great Society Architectural Planning Center; "Bank Operations" at the Girard Trust Bank; and "Basic Electricity" at the Philadelphia Gas Works. Because of logistics of scheduling and transportation arrangements, the outside courses did not begin all at once, but rather over roughly a two-week period*

Although the outside program had successfully involved a wide range of businesses and institutions in the Community Free School program, three difficult problems still faced the community coordinator: first, to arrange with teachers and students a satisfactory procedure for rostering students into the course or courses of their choice; secondly, to set up adequate means of transportation to and from the school and outside course sites; third, to overcome student hesitancy, anxiety, and fear in regard to the program itself. While the first two problems were worked out as the program was implemented, the problem of student unfamiliarity and apprehension was more fundamental and hard to overcome. These and other problematic aspects of the outside program will be discussed in the chapter, "Reflections on the Implementation Process."

Most of the outside course instructors did not know what to expect from the program. They were unfamiliar with the world of the schools, even less so with an innovative school. In order to help acquaint the instructors with the Community Free School and its students, several opportunities were taken to bring them into the school building. In the course of three meetings scheduled during the first term, outside course instructors met with the Community Free School teachers on an informal basis, sharing their concerns and experiences with the professional staff. These meetings were necessarily limited in duration and frequency, because the professional staff had heavy workloads and the outside course instructors held full time commitments to their jobs. In addition to these orientation and evaluation meetings, the instructors were also provided with ongoing support through the community coordinator's office.

Staff Development

The teacher in the Community Free School was expected to be a guide in the learning process in addition to being a counselor for the

---

*See Appendix for descriptions of representative outside courses.

students in his family group. The Community Free School student, then was considered responsible for his own education, in that he was expected at some point to take the initiative in expressing his own desires and ideas. Naturally, students coming from years of traditional schooling in the inner city could not be expected to develop these independent abilities overnight. Nevertheless, during the initial months of the school's operation, teachers were disappointed at the apparent lack of student motivation.

Unable to rely on students to the extent they had anticipated and unwilling to fill the gap by assuming a more traditional authoritarian role, teachers were uncertain and confused. One teacher noted that several colleagues were experiencing real anguish and that this was interfering with communication between teachers and students. In their confusion, teachers naturally turned to each other as the most logical and accessible source of help.

Teacher interaction was critically important during the first phase, because it allowed teachers to share their initial experiences and deal with their frustrations and accomplishments as a group. Once a teacher realized that his problems were not unique, the personal anguish and self-doubt were somewhat relieved. Teacher interaction provided a positive means of locating the source of a problem, defining its nature and extent, and searching for a solution. Needless to say, interaction also contributed to a feeling of cohesiveness and community among teachers in the school.

After the first month, interaction between teachers, students and staff became the primary process for decision making and the basic operating principle of the Community Free School, within the educational program as well as in administrative matters. Teachers worked together in planning, teaching, and evaluating their classes; students also joined teachers in planning and evaluating courses. During the first semester over 75% of combined teaching hours were spent in teams. There were many different team combinations. For example: one certified teacher might join two graduate interns and teach a class of 35 students; or two certified teachers would work with 25 to 35 students, with the assistance of two student teachers. A basic characteristic of all teaching teams was their flexibility: teacher groupings remained very fluid; some teachers moved in and out of teams every few weeks; others would sit in on a variety of classes, informally helping teachers in other teams. This degree of interaction was possible because of the small school environment — every teacher knew what every other teacher was doing.

After the first month of family group meetings and the inter-disciplinary theme project, teachers and students began working on course subjects within the disciplines of science, mathematics, humanities and social science. The Community Free School curriculum focused on the mastery of basic skills through individual and small group instruction. Teachers and staff planned the courses themselves, with help from individual students. In an informal way, these students began to take a greater part in planning than they had during the first weeks. Since teachers were not relying on textbooks and lesson plans, they were very open to each other and to student assistance and students' reactions to the curriculum. At the end of the first semester, the teaching staff had developed into an effective and flexible working unit. Firm relationships had been established among teachers and students. One teacher noted in June the differences he perceived from his earlier experiences at West Philadelphia High School:

> Other schools create barriers which impede dialogues between teachers and students, students and students, and teachers and teachers . . . they provide little or no opportunity for teachers to work together in developing curriculum, sharing problems and successes, or coordinating activities which meet the needs of particular students . . . I have seen all three types of interchange occur at the Community Free School.

Student Development

The student in the Community Free School faced many new experiences and challenges. Many students had difficulty adjusting to the open environment, the increased options available to them, and the new responsibility which was extended to them. In the course of the first semester, students began slowly to respond constructively to the educational program, to assume a legitimate role in the school community, and to take responsibility for their own education.

During the first week of school a student steering committee consisting of four to five students from different family groups and of one teacher was organized. Student representatives were elected in family group meetings. Besides acting as representatives of student concerns, the steering committee members acted in several other capacities during the first semester. They participated in teacher and administrative staff meetings, attended community board meetings, joined teachers in developing the inside educational program for the Community Free School, and offered their own evaluations of the curriculum as well as that of their fellow students. While the steering committee was not always truly representative in its actions, and while its effectiveness as a policy-making body fluctuated, it did present students with many opportunities to demonstrate that the Community Free School was indeed partly student-run.

One of the most significant actions taken by the Steering Committee concerned student discipline. Attendance records from the beginning of the year showed absences from class approaching 20% on some days, although absenteeism from school itself was minimal. Class cutting rather than truancy was clearly the problem, as some students misinterpreted "freedom" and misused their free time periods. Yet while staff concern over the problem grew, so did student concern. Teachers told members of the steering committee that the Community Free School was their school, and that this problem was theirs to handle. Naturally, no one student wanted to be in a position of "spying" on or "judging" his fellow students and friends; however, several weeks after school opened, the steering committee reluctantly appointed a judicial board of students to deal with the problem of class cutting and other disciplinary matters. The judicial board, like the steering committee, has fluctuated in its effectiveness. Yet both organizations remained student-initiated and student-run, and their decisions continued to form a part of Community Free School policy during the first semester. By insisting students assume this responsibility, teachers encouraged students to take responsibility for their own education and for their fellow students.

In contrast to the attitude which they had exhibited before enrollment in the Community Free School, the students were extremely protective of their new school houses. They would tolerate no vandalism in their buildings, and when outsiders entered and caused destruction, the students took great pains to restore their house. (In one instance, students repainted the entranceway three times to cover graffiti which neighborhood gang members had sprayed on the walls.)

This attitude of pride and responsibility for their environment carried over into their behavior in outside programs where few complaints of vandalism by the students were reported.

One incident, seemingly of student irresponsibility, must be mentioned as it is illustrative of problems which may arise. Local merchants, specifically restauranteurs and grocers, registered numerous complaints of shoplifting by students to the administration of the school. The reason for these thefts was a puzzle to the staff until it was discovered that a student's lunch ran approximately $1.50 per day, as there were no cafeteria facilities or accommodations for eating within the houses. The strain of producing this amount of money daily exceeded the economic capabilities of most Free School students. Therefore, many saw shoplifting as their only resource. This problem was resolved for one house when parents and community members, in an exemplary manifestation of unity, organized an in-house lunch program, which helped to alleviate the lunch-time theft problem.

Because of the individualized and nongraded educational program, students at the Community Free School didn't feel pressure to compete for positions in a "class-ranking." Students were able to begin learning at their own level of competence; they were allowed to fail and try again, with no stigma attached to the failure. In many cases, student interest in school and learning revived in this atmosphere. One student explained it in this way:

> If it hadn't been for the Community Free School, I would have dropped out. I couldn't stand the "A," "B" pressure. If we had grades here, I'd be right on top; I'd be just average at West Philadelphia High School. I work harder here because I'm doing things I want to do.

By the time of the first graduation exercises, in June 1970, 20% of the first graduating class had decided to spend an extra year at the Community Free School. Although they could have received their diplomas, these students felt that they needed more preparation for their lives beyond high school.

The interest which students demonstrated represents the kind of involvement which is possible only in a school which is also a community of individuals who trust and respect one another. Perhaps the most promising aspect of the Community Free School during Phase I was the development of honest and open relationships among students, teachers, and staff. In an essay on the Community Free School, a student expressed this feeling as follows:

> As a whole the Community Free School is people growing mentally and working hard together. It's getting inside and outside knowledge. Most of all, it's teachers helping you and you helping them . . . Our school is different from others because it's a device that brings togetherness, whether you're black or white.

Process Evaluation

Because the Community Free School was an innovative venture, there were few precedents teachers and staff could rely upon to guide them through the first months of the implementation process. As already noted, the newness of the program served to draw teachers together, they depended upon one another for support and advice to a great extent because there was very little benefit they could gain from procedures and guidelines of traditional high school institutions. In much the same way, teachers and staff of the Community Free School evaluated their own performance in the school in terms of the goals of the model, their personal goals for the school, and the overall development of the project, rather than based on standards or criteria established outside the environment of the school itself. In addition, the results of evaluations were communicated to those involved in the program as soon as they were available along with suggestions for solutions to problems and advice. The two-way flow of information, which was established during Phase I and which was perpetuated and expanded in later semesters, might be called "process evaluation."

Evaluation of the inside program was generated by the teachers. Teachers were asked to keep field notes which they passed in at intervals during the first semester. Regular teacher meetings were scheduled, which were attended by some students and often by community board members. These meetings were intended to deal with any problems which arose during the implementation process, and to evaluate in detail the procedures and structure of the Community Free School. In addition to these meetings, several group interviews with students, teachers, and community board members were scheduled during the first semester. During these interviews the implementation process was discussed in relation to the theory of the model, and the participants sought to gain a greater perspective of the school as a whole.

Evaluation of the outside program was less extensive and ongoing than that of the inside program. On three occasions, outside course instructors were invited to the school for informal meetings with the professional teaching staff. During these meetings, the instructors began to evaluate their experiences in detail and to get immediate feedback from the professional teachers. The community coordinator remained accessible to the outside course instructors throughout the semester. Although he did make visits to outside course classrooms, he was not able to visit all of them. Instead, communications would be carried out by telephone and, in some cases, by tape-recording.

PHASE III: EXPANSION AND REFINEMENT

During the spring and summer, the community board and the staff of the Community Free School planned for expansion from one to three houses, raising the student body from 200 to 500. Besides replicating the program in additional scattered sites, we were anxious to refine many elements of the school's structure and procedures on the basis of our experiences during the first semester. Expansion and refinement were thus simultaneous concerns during Phase III. Much of the program developed during the first and second phases was sustained during Phase III. Rather than describe these aspects of the program for a second time, we will concentrate instead on those issues related to expansion and refinement.

The Programs

At the end of the first semester of the Community Free School's operation, teachers and staff had met to evaluate the inside educational program, to discuss plans for expansion into three houses, and to determine what aspects of the program needed to be changed and how they could be most effectively refined or altered. The general comments and specific suggestions which came out of these meetings

47

WEST PHILADELPHIA
COMMUNITY FREE SCHOOL

(Expansion to Three Locations)

3833 Walnut St.

3625 Walnut St.

4226 Baltimore Ave.

were used in planning the educational programs for the three houses during the summer and for the teacher training workshop in the fall.

One of the principal criticisms teachers raised in relation to the first semester concerned the interdisciplinary theme project, the environmental box. Teachers felt that the project had not fully realized its potential for several reasons. First, it operated for a short period of time and was introduced to students when the school environment was still very new to them; consequently, there was much confusion among students — confusion which also created problems for the teachers in determining what they could expect from the students in their family groups. Secondly, the organization of the box project had, to a large extent, been left up to teachers and students. Because there was not a great deal of time available for planning and because of the many other organizational details and problems which teachers inevitably faced during the first weeks of school, the loose structure of the project resulted in a somewhat haphazard educational experience — some student projects went very well while others were never clearly organized or never materialized at all. Finally, teachers expressed their concern that the activities and projects which were carried out during the first several weeks did not sufficiently identify student ability levels nor relate clearly enough to the inside educational program which began after the first month. While they still favored all-day family group meetings during an initial transitional period, teachers were anxious to provide students with an introduction to basic skills activities and concrete aspects of the educational program at the same time.

As a result of these teacher evaluations and the teacher training workshop, plans for the first month of school were substantially refined for the fall semester. The interdisciplinary box was discarded; instead, teachers working in teams during the summer training workshop developed their own plans for the all-day family group meetings. The objectives were several: (1) to enable students and teachers to get to know each other, (2) to enable teachers to identify student interests and ability levels (3) to set up the three house organizations, e.g., committees, criteria for attendance, evaluations, credit (4) to decorate and renovate the house facility, and (5) to introduce students to the basic skills curriculum.

While students and teachers were still meeting all day in family groups, another new aspect of the program was established and implemented. A reading and a writing workshop was designed as an additional activity during the first transitional month, to provide continuity between the initial weeks and the rest of the school year. The workshop was located in a large open area in each of the three houses. Workshop projects consisted of individual and small group activities, dealing with vocabulary building, independent and directed reading, and writing skills. There were many structured activities although independent work was always encouraged. Materials and resources in the workshop space included a house library, word games and puzzles, and a wealth of exercises designed by teachers in the house. Each student and humanities teacher in the house spent between two and four hours every week in the workshop, rotating in and out as their schedules permitted. An average workshop consisted of two teachers and 25 to 30 students. Student work was kept in individual folders, which were stored in a central file in each workshop and which were always accessible to students and teachers. The reading and writing workshops enabled teachers to determine quickly student ability levels and keep track of their development. They turned out to be an extremely successful innovation during Phase III and rapidly became the core of the humanities program in each house.

On the recommendation of teachers and students, humanities, social studies, science and language classes were also shortened and varied in duration from an hour to an hour and a half. In addition, we introduced four to six-week "minicourses" to the curriculum of each house. Teachers from different disciplines would join in teaching an interdisciplinary minicourse such as "The Role of Women" or "Ways of Knowing," (personal psychology). In planning and evaluating these courses, teachers also drew on the expertise of colleagues from different disciplines. The shorter courses permitted teachers to develop a more varied curriculum and also offered students a greater range of choices.*

The inside educational program remained flexible throughout Phase III; student rosters were revised several times during the semester. (A sample roster, see Appendix, indicates the variety of experiences we were able to offer students during this phase of the implementation.)

---

*See Appendix for short descriptions of some minicourses.

Test Coaching: The SAT coaching program, which was set up during the first semester with the help of the Educational Testing Service, was expanded during Phase III. When the Community Free School opened in the fall, the program began running in all three houses. The program consisted of two parts, verbal and math coaching. One teacher in each reading and writing workshop supervised a verbal coaching program. Eighty-two students chose to participate in the program; they worked at their own rate in test-coaching workbooks provided by ETS and recorded their progress on charts placed in their workshop folders for this purpose. A math coaching program was set up in the math workshop periods, and one math teacher in each house supervised student progress in these workbooks. In both programs, teachers encouraged seniors to work at a faster rate than the others because they would be taking the SAT's early in the year at the University of Pennsylvania.

The SAT was administered to approximately 60 seniors in mid-December. Special arrangements had been made with ETS to encourage the students to relax as much as possible since tests of this type tend to create much anxiety which may affect students' scores negatively. We spoke to the students before the test, explaining that while some rules were being relaxed, the validity of the test results would be jeopardized if minimal standards were not maintained. During the administration, Community Free School teachers dropped by to help supervise the room and circulated among the students; their presence was reassuring to the students who were faced with this new and difficult challenge. In the middle of the test a break was scheduled, during which students were served refreshments; this was a great success, and helped them to keep working until the test was over.*

---

*The score results from the SAT administration indicated an average gain of 40 points over previous SAT and PSAT scores. While these results are neither dramatic nor conclusive, neither do they indicate that test-coaching programs such as this should be abandoned. Experimental test-coaching programs to date have not demonstrated that this will ultimately prove to be the correct approach, but they have not disproved the possibility. Because the SAT's remain such an important factor in determining a student's future, they must be given every opportunity to improve their scores on this test. For this reason alone we believe test coaching programs should be continued wherever necessary. A critical problem remains, though, as to whether to continue trying to "adapt" students to the SAT's — coaching them in test taking skills for the sake of maintaining a standard, nationwide measurement of student ability — or to begin adapting the SAT to the student, dealing with social, cultural and ethnic differences in a positive way by means of varied and specialized testing. Perhaps the latter method will, if universally adopted, provide more equitable and effective means of reaching students from every area and background who are themselves beginning to reach for positive goals.

Staff Development

The expanded teaching staff of the Community Free School was selected during May and June by a committee consisting of community board members, the directors, students, and members of the original teaching staff. Nearly all of the original teachers, including the graduate interns, had requested reappointment to the Community Free School for the next year. Consequently, the enlarged teaching staff consisted of 20 certified teachers, eight of the originally certified teachers, eight newly certified teachers, four former graduate interns who were now fully certified; a new group of twelve graduate interns, six student teachers; and six community teachers. On the basis of the training activities which were carried out during Phase I and in order to draw on the experiences of returning teachers and other staff, it was determined during Phase II to conduct an extensive training workshop for the entire teaching staff.

The teacher training workshop was conducted over a two-week period directly preceding the fall semester. All of the teachers were asked to attend, and students and community members were also an integral part of the workshop. All-day training sessions were held in the house. Teachers, students, and community members also took field trips and worked on group projects in the community. The purpose of the training workshop was threefold: first, to introduce all members of the school community to one another and to involve them in projects in which they could learn about each other as individuals and as partners in the learning process; second, to orient new teachers to the goals and structure of the Community Free School and to introduce them to the methods, resources, learning situations, and group interaction of the educational program; third, to orient the teachers to the geographical community and to familiarize them with the needs and concerns of that community. Throughout the workshop the primary emphasis was on the learning-teaching process rather than on developing specific course content or resource materials.

The project experiences of the workshop were designed to fall into two basic areas. The first group of activities was structured: participants were given instructions or assignments and were asked to develop their own solutions by working together and by themselves. The second type of activity was less structured: informal meetings and group discussions were encouraged, and the guidelines offered were broader and allowed more independent initiative. A brief outline of the activities within these two groups follows.

Structured Activities

Teacher Discussions: Teachers were divided into three groups; each group contained certified teachers, graduate students and Community Teachers. Questions raised during the discussions were:

— How do you perceive your role in the West Philadelphia Community Free School?

— What do you expect from your students?

— What changes in teacher and student attitude do you predict in the course of the year?

— What do you hope to accomplish in this new learning situation?

Each discussion was videotaped. In the afternoon, the tapes were projected among the groups, and the same issues were raised in this new context. Teachers analyzed the situation they had faced in the morning and discussed how and why some of them reacted the way they did.

Teacher Portraits: Teachers were paired off, each with a tape-recorder. They were asked to "interview" each other, to explore their ideas, attitudes and experiences on a one-to-one basis.

Student-Teacher Portraits: Students and teachers worked together in groups of three. They tape-recorded their discussions, much as the teachers had done several days before.

Microteaching: Teachers were given an assignment: design an activity for the opening day of the Community Free School. Teachers paired off and worked out an idea which they demonstrated with the help of students and fellow-teachers in a five-minute class. Each performance was videotaped, then played back for group analysis and evaluation directly afterward. At the end of the workshop, each pair of teachers presented a written outline of the 'objectives' and 'procedure' of the activity, revised in light of criticism offered.

Space Allocation: Separating into small groups, teachers and students visited the three houses (renovated residential and commercial buildings) which comprise the Community Free School. They drew up floor-plans, then assigned space within each house to different study areas such as science, humanities (library, workshop), mathematics (laboratory), and recreation. The plans were enlarged and displayed, then analyzed and contrasted by teachers, students and community participants.

Community Mapping: Equipped with Polaroid cameras, note-books and tape recorders, small groups of teachers and students combed the areas surrounding the Community Free School, surveying residential areas and business districts. Each group compiled a list of points of interest in the community; these included restaurants, food stores, university facilities, book stores and other shops, museums, libraries, hospitals, community centers, recreation facilities, amusement centers — in short, all community institutions and enterprises relevant to the interests and needs of the Community Free School teacher and student.

Media Workshops: Rotating groups of teachers and students worked with media specialists, exploring uses of the tape recorder, movie and video cameras, and methods of nonverbal communication.

Nonstructured Activities

Community Visits: Several times during the workshop, teachers left the school to visit a community organization. Members of the school's community board led discussions on the role of the community in education and accompanied teachers on tours of healthy and depressed areas of the community. Throughout the workshop, community board members and teachers shared their observations, experiences and expectations.

Group Work: In the course of the workshop, the teaching staff was subdivided into three groups, one for each of the three houses. Teachers within each group began to work together, during free hours, to develop a plan for the first weeks of school when students and teachers would work together outside of the classroom in family groups. As the workshop progressed, teachers devoted more time to house-team-planning, sometimes working in the evening on ideas and suggestions raised during the day. Beyond the general guidelines, there were no restrictions placed on this activity; teachers were able to move in any direction they chose. Consequently, they worked closely together, depending on each other for ideas and feedback. Many of the proposals teachers made during these informal meetings drew on the experiences of the more structured workshop activities, e.g., micro-teaching, tape recorded portraits, field trips.*

During the group planning sessions, teachers began to work together as a team, and a feeling of mutual trust and shared enthusiasm forged a bond between teachers which would enable them to deal flexibly with the coming year. The variety of proposals presented at the end of the workshop showed that teachers realized there was more than one way to approach a learning situation.

TEACHER TRAINING WORKSHOP
SCHEDULE OF PROJECT EXPERIENCES

	Monday	Tuesday	Wednesday	Thursday	Friday
a.m.	Introduction	Teacher Portraits		Space Allocation	Micro teaching
	Videotaped Discussion	Media Workshops			
p.m.	Videotape Review	Videotape Review	Group Work	Student-Teacher Portraits	Group Work
eve.			Community Visit		

	Saturday	Sunday	Monday	Tuesday	Wednesday
a.m.	Community Visit		Community Mapping		Presentation: Results of Group Work
p.m.	Group Work			Group Work	Conclusion

*When family groups began to meet, some of the workshop activities were applied directly in the family group meetings and field trips, e.g., space allocation, community mapping.

Though evaluation of the teacher training workshop was thus an ongoing process, there were special times set aside for a more formal analysis of the program. Those students involved in the workshop met for a short period of time at the end of each day to discuss what had happened and how to improve upon it. Teachers spent two hours per day evaluating — with the help of community trainees — what they had done and deciding which activities should be given greater emphasis in future sessions. Students were, of course, encouraged to participate and did participate in these meetings.

Most of the teachers felt that the media workshop was the least worthwhile activity, as it was too disorganized. One participant stated that it was "useful only in that it demonstrated how the lack of clarity in presentation and purpose could lead to extreme frustration and failure of a good idea."

Most of the teachers reacted favorably to the videotaping as a means of "breaking the ice," encouraging discussion, and evaluating changes within and among teachers. Most teachers felt that the time spent on space allocation encouraged participants to work together and provided for a variety of inputs. Students-teacher portraits were also felt to be useful in helping people get to know one another and in developing interview techniques. Of the community mapping activity, one teacher said, "Very good, opened my mind to a new way of looking at the community, not just as a source of problems but as an area filled with resources for us to use." Many felt that microteaching was the highlight of the training program since many ideas were presented, a feeling of working together was accomplished, and a supportive atmosphere for experimentation was developed. All felt that group work was a good way to build strong interpersonal relations among teachers and individual self-confidence. Teachers' suggestions for improvement of teacher training workshops were: shorten to two weeks, eliminate things that didn't work out well, and don't embark on space allocation or group work until houses are assigned.

The evaluation processes in the school, of course, continued while the school was in session. Teachers sometimes taped their actual lessons and these were shown in the weekly critique sessions which were conducted at the University. These tapes were played back in the houses themselves, thus enabling the students to take part in the evaluation process as well.

The short minicourses, the varied programs within the reading and writing workshops, and the expansion of interdisciplinary curricula enabled teachers to work simultaneously in several teaching situations during Phase III. In the course of the second semester at the Community Free School, teachers worked in teams and as individuals within and between disciplines and with small and larger groups of students. An example of one teacher's weekly schedule (See "Typical Days", p. 101) during the second semester illustrates the variety of teaching experiences and team combinations which were possible in this environment. Through a process of adaptation and refinement, teachers developed curricula and teaching methods which responded to the needs of individual students, enabled both teachers and students to keep track of course development and student progress, and sustained the involvement of all participants in working together as a planning and teaching team.

Student Development

Teachers' meetings remained open to students, and the student steering committee and judicial board continued to function in all three houses. During Phase III, students, in several concrete cases, demonstrated a growing concern with the structure and program of the school. At one point, steering committee representatives and several other students in one of the houses approached their teachers with specific complaints relating to the reading and writing workshop in their house. A meeting was called, and students and teachers discussed specific problems and recommendations. The workshop was subsequently restructured and during the second semester, students were asked to comment on the first semester's curriculum. In their written evaluations, students candidly and critically assessed their classes. Teachers used student comments and recommendations in planning for the third semester. On another occasion, the students in one house requested a meeting with teachers to discuss teaching and curriculum content. A lively discussion and debate took place, and specific proposals were ultimately adopted. These and other examples indicate that students in the Community Free School were growing more confident in the new environment, that they were beginning to deal with problems and to participate actively in and share the responsibility for the development of their school's educational program.

Process Evaluation

The expanded program of the Community Free School represented a test of the PASS Model and of the effectiveness of the first two phases of the implementation process. Two new facilities were acquired; the teaching staff and student body of the school nearly tripled; the outside course program expanded to eighty courses, and the community coordinator's office now had to arrange for scheduling and transportation to and from the outside course sites and the three scattered school sites. The original teaching staff was divided into three core teams, one for each house.

Perhaps expansion went ahead too quickly. In many respects there was not enough preparation to implement the program on an expanded scale. On the one hand, the three houses were set up and did operate on a day-to-day basis; within the house, the teachers and students experienced greater autonomy in the second semester than during the first semester. Each house developed a unique character and program while adhering to the basic educational goals and structures of the PASS Model.

On the other hand, the process of running three schools and the problems related to the expansion of the program often took precedence over refining the structure and educational program. In many cases the same difficulties and problems experienced in implementing one house during Phase I and II were now faced, only on a larger scale. The following chapter will describe these problems in detail and will present recommendations for avoiding and/or overcoming them. Awareness of "what to look out for" when implementing an alternative community school is a valuable asset to anyone attempting a similar project, for it is by learning from the experience of others that these problems may be overcome in the future.

CHAPTER III

**REFLECTIONS ON THE
IMPLEMENTATION PROCESS**

REFLECTIONS ON THE IMPLEMENTATION PROCESS

The following section is not a formal evaluation of the Community Free School implementation process, nor is it a detailed discussion of specific issues. Rather, it consists of a review of and reflection on the implementation process and the participants in it. By so doing, we touch on many issues that were problematic in the process, discuss the implications and results of decisions that were made, and, finally, deal with the interrelationships among the partners and their involvement in the process.

The section has three major divisions:

1. Community Participation: the partnership concept and the activities and involvement of each partner.

2. The School Community: issues involved in the new roles of teachers and students.

3. The Educational Program: its development in relation to students, teachers, and the operation of the school as a whole.

COMMUNITY PARTICIPATION

The partnership of community, public education, university, and local business and industry is fundamental to the operation of a school such as the Community Free School. The problems of the urban community in general and of urban education in particular are such that no one institution can hope to deal with them alone. The resources of the urban community are of enormous value to education, and only through cooperation among a number of different institutions can teachers and students have access to these resources.

The concept of a partnership also highlights the need for all interest groups within the urban community to take responsibility for the improvement of educational institutions — institutions from which they receive benefits of many kinds, not the least of which is a constant supply of manpower. Only through such a partnership can public education be responsive to all groups within the community in that each makes inputs into the educational decision-making process.

"West Philadelphia is a large and diverse community whose problems are those facing all urban areas in the United States, not the least of which is public education. The problems of education are indeed critical as the public school system is one institution in the community which has the inherent capacity to set long range goals and provide for change. At the present facilities are grossly inadequate: buildings are outdated, overcrowded, and plagued by vandalism. The dropout rate is high, and a good percentage of those who do graduate cannot read or write sufficiently well to enter the job market at other than low levels. Teachers as well as students and community members are highly dissatisfied with educational facilities and conditions in Philadelphia.

"Some residents of West Philadelphia are able to spare themselves and their children from the problems of the public system. These are the whites and the few blacks who can afford to send their children to private and parochial schools. The majority of blacks, however, do not have this option because they cannot afford the price of private education. Consequently, these parents have no alternative but to send their children to the public schools where, if they are lucky and conscientious despite overwhelming odds, they will learn the minimal skills necessary to find employment or to enter college or other post-high school training.

"These are the public schools. The institutions of higher learning in West Philadelphia also face problems of money and facilities. Their traditional role has been that of research and the training of scholars and professionals. To that end, universities throughout the country have been expanding their facilities at a rapid rate to meet the increased demand for higher education. In urban areas, this means expansion into the residential community, tearing down homes and other facilities to provide for the university community. Residents thus see the traditional goals of the university in conflict with their own. Witness the battle over the Morningside Heights gymnasium at Columbia University. The complaint of the residential community is that housing facilities have been torn down, but no new housing has been constructed, that the urban university has not applied its expertise, facilities, and personnel in any substantial way to alleviating the critical problems of the city. The university has engaged in small scale community projects, but as yet has made no large inroads into the problems of metropolitan areas.

"Business and industry in the urban community are subject to similar criticisms in that they have not turned their profits back into the community in such a way as to improve the living and working conditions of city residents. Business, however, also reaps the disadvantages created by the cycle of urban problems. The inadequacy of educational facilities and the consequent ineffectiveness of the schools means that business must often go outside the community in search of capable employees. More and more industries are moving out of the city in search of lower tax and wage rates and less political pressure. Those industries which do remain and do feel a commitment to the community are perplexed as to what their role should be in helping to solve urban problems."*

While we firmly believe that the notion of partnership in education is a fundamentally sound and feasible one, the realities of urban life and urban education made it difficult to achieve in the case of the Community Free School. This section will detail the responsibilities, activities and limitations of each of the partners in the alternative school.

---

*Aase Eriksen, *Scattered Schools*, pp. 12 and 14

The Community Board

The community board, composed as it is of representatives of all the partners in the project, is the chief decision-making body in the Community Free School. Community residents, however, rather than institutional representatives, make up the majority of members. It was these community people who first initiated the action which led to the creation of the school and who originally met with university representatives, the principal of West Philadelphia High School, the district superintendent, and the superintendent of schools. During Phase I, community members and the staff continued to meet with these officials to interview and select personnel for the school. They also explained the aims and program of the school to the business community, the parents and the students and encouraged them to participate in the new endeavor.

It later became apparent, however, that after the major logistic problems of implementing this experimental school had been solved, community residents who were members of the community board began to see their role as supervisory and the successful operation of the school program as a foregone conclusion. As a consequence, they became less visible in the school, more reluctant to deal with problems of the program's operation, and less accessible to all participants including students and teachers. While teachers looked to the community board, for example, for help in solving daily problems, community board members felt the daily operation of the school and the educational program were the responsibility of the director and teachers. However, community board members were unwilling to surrender the necessary decision-making authority to the director and teachers; at the same time, the teachers were hesitant to make decisions because they interpreted literally the concept of community involvement in the school. Therefore, decisions concerning the daily operation of the school were at times at a stalemate.

This conflict points to a more basic consideration for starting and developing a community school. It must be decided at the outset whether it will be a school run by a community board only or a school that is itself a community. If the second conception is chosen, then, once the school is established according to the wishes of the community, a new community consisting of all active participants in the school also comes into being. It is of primary importance that all members of this school community share in the decision-making process. While at times expediency may require quick decisions on the part of one or two people, participants must be continually conscious of the need to maintain the democratic decision-making process. For, in a school of this size, democracy can function. All must, therefore, be willing to accept the frustrations and delays that accompany this sharing of responsibility and the gathering of the input of all concerned members of the school community. This model of a community school also implies that all participants, not only community residents or students, have a serious stake in the success of the school.

It has been our experience that, unless this democratic consciousness is shared by all participants (if, indeed, that is the goal of the school), there is a tendency in the community school for decision-making to fall into the hands of a single group and for that group, by its then authoritarian nature, to revert to bureaucratic rather than democratic procedures. Thus, in the Community Free School, community residents felt the school was one over which *they* had control while staff and teachers felt the school was itself intended to be a democratic community. Thus, occurred the reluctance of the board to share the frustrations of the teachers and help alleviate their daily problems and, on the other hand, the teachers' growing disillusionment with the community board's role in the project. More specifically, while the board was reluctant to help solve the daily problems of the school's operation and consult with teachers on an equal footing regarding such matters, they were unwilling, at the same time, to allow teachers the authority to do so themselves.

Both conceptions of a community school are feasible, but the participants must be sure at the very beginning that all share and adhere to the choice that has been made. Failing such agreement, it seems inevitable that conflict will ensue at the most basic level of policy and operation — conflict which undermines all aspects of the implementation as well as the ultimate success of a community school.

The model and the Community Free School itself must in the final analysis be considered the "property" of the community board, and it is the community group at the head of the school which must change the model if they see fit or if their desires or needs change. Yet, in order to give an alternative school a fair chance and to allow a period of experimentation to determine whether the goals can be reached, the community must also engage in the process of implementation.

Community board members must allow a period of transition (even approaching seeming chaos) to take place and must allow the necessary changes to be made as the school moves towards its objectives. Moreover, in their own policy and decision-making, the community should arrive at solutions by dealing with individuals and circumstances without fear of change or of making mistakes. They must avoid the establishment of rules and procedures which make the school static and thus unresponsive to the very people it is meant to serve.

The Business Advisory Board

In the spring of 1970 the business advisory board was formed. Its members were the presidents and vice presidents of local business and industrial firms, including, for example, several major Philadelphia banks and utility companies. Approximately fifteen companies were represented on the board.

The business advisory board functioned most effectively during the first six months of its existence. It was originally organized to act as a liaison between the Community Free School and the business community in order to involve other businesses in the educational program. The board later expanded its responsibilities to include:

1. Working with the ongoing design of new kinds of courses and projects;

2. Helping to organize and support an ongoing teacher training program for the teachers from business and industry;

3. Involving business and other organizations in the program;

4. Helping to raise funds for the additional expenditures of the outside course program;

5. Using their influence to facilitate and support the alternative program of the Community Free School in any way possible.

It was during this initial operating period of the business advisory board that the enthusiasm for the Community Free School project was at its peak among the board members and as a result a great deal was accomplished. The outside course program was expanded to include a wider variety of courses in more local businesses and institutions. The board succeeded in raising some $20,000 by means of a fund-raising drive to support the office and staff of the outside program course coordinator while negotiations were underway with the board of education to fund this office internally. The most effective board action was the role it played in helping the board of education fulfill its obligations. As explained earlier, the Community Free School ran into serious problems when permission was first sought from the city zoning board to convert a row house into a school building. Permission was at first denied, largely on the basis of an inadequate presentation of the case to the zoning board. Furthermore, delays in the renovation of the unit in accordance with the requirements of the zoning board and the city building code resulted from the board of education's delay in selecting a contractor. At this point, members of the business advisory board used their influence to speed the selection and renovation process to ensure that the building would be ready for occupancy for the coming school year. In addition, when the renovations were completed, parents and other members of the community attended the second zoning board hearing to plead the case for the Community Free School. The zoning board then approved the building for occupancy by the Community Free School, and students and teachers moved into the building within a week.

However, this high level of involvement and activity by the business advisory board was not sustained, and attendance at the board meetings dropped as interest waned. An important reason for the turn of events was that the business advisory board was never made an integral part of the community board. Although the chairman of the business board was invited to attend community board meetings as an observer, he was never permitted to become a voting member. Moreover, the lack of adequate and trained staff in the community coordinator's office led to inadequate support and advice to business board members and teachers from the business community.

The result was that every month a group of men and women met in the conference room of a local bank to discuss their involvement in the Community Free School in a static environment remote from the actual operation of the school which was itself dynamic and undergoing constant change. To be effective in the long run, a group like the business advisory board must play an integral role in the operation of the school. Members who are willing to devote their time and energy as well as the resources of their organization to fulfilling the responsibilities outlined for the business advisory board must be given the opportunity to do so.

The University

The Community Free School was itself the result of community pressure on the university to take responsibility for the improvement of the community of which it is a part. The University of Pennsylvania responded to the demands of the community by the contribution of essential implementation funds, personnel and facilities.

The stated role of the University in the West Philadelphia Community Free School model was to act as an educational resource as well as a guide and lever for the community in helping them achieve their aims for the education of their children. In order to do so, the president and provost personally called on members of the business community to contribute their support and to involve themselves in the outside program. Luncheons were held where businessmen received information about the Community Free School project and where they learned what their role could be in its successful implementation.

The university further contributed the services of the director of the Community Free School as well as the services of administrative personnel to work with the community board, the board of education, and the business community. It was through the university's original loan as well as through the work of its personnel that additional monies were acquired to keep the Community Free School in operation during its first two years.

Graduate interns and undergraduate student teachers from the university were essential to the continuing operation of the Community Free School program in that they reduced the student-teacher ratio to the level necessary to give students the individualized instruction in the basic skills which they sorely needed. The university originally provided the funding for the community teachers who helped to reduce the student-teacher ratio, offered a wider variety of courses to students, and acted as the community's liaison in the school. Many other university volunteers, both students and faculty, worked technically in the outside program and offered West Philadelphia Community Free School students courses they would not otherwise have had the opportunity to take. In addition, some Community Free School students participated in regular undergraduate courses given to university students.

Other necessary services, generally provided by the board of education in public schools, fell to the lot of the university. Interns in the Graduate School of Social Work offered their services to the Community Free School as did other university related tutoring and counseling programs. A staff member of the school of education spent full time, while being paid as a half time assistant, to insure the smooth operation and success of the outside program. The university registrar contributed computer time and man hours to facilitating the rostering of Community Free School courses.

University facilities and equipment were frequently used (and sometimes at a rental cost) for such activities as SAT administration, student production, all school meetings, and teacher training sessions. The Computer Center loaned three Datel terminals at nominal cost for the math program. In addition, the frequent delays encountered in acquiring equipment, furniture, teaching materials, and supplies necessitated the expenditure of funds from the university budget to get standard board of education supplies. Even furniture had to be rented so that students would have adequate facilities with which to work. The university budget, moreover, paid for much of the renovation and maintenance of the Community Free School buildings through the use of personnel from the Department of Buildings and Grounds.

The university's contribution to the West Philadelphia Community Free School, then, went far beyond the original commitment of guidance, leverage and material support for those extras involved in the implementation of an innovative educational program. University personnel were consistently supportive of the program and unhesitatingly used university funds when necessary to acquire the standard equipment and materials that were so often delayed by procedural and other practices of the board of education.

Despite the obvious commitment and contributions of the university to the implementation and operation of the Community Free School, the university as an institution was, in some ways, limited by its very nature and structure. In the final analysis, one of its greatest contributions was in terms of students rather than faculty and other personnel who had more specialized skills and knowledge to offer to Free School students and teachers. Moreover, while a school or department of education is obviously one of the most important resources the university has to offer for the improvement of public education, it is often the case that departments of education are more concerned with establishing their legitimacy within the academic structure of the university rather than with improving the public education system. Involvement in real and complex problems of education carries less prestige and is often felt by academicians to inhibit objectivity and scholarly attitudes. The Community Free School received from the Graduate School of Education of the University of Pennsylvania student teachers and graduate interns to help staff the school. While this is not a small contribution, it was only gained at the continued insistence of two professors of education within the school. Had more support been forthcoming — in terms of evaluation, curriculum development, consultation, and moral — the implementation of the Community Free School would have been less problematic and the university's overall support (and position in the alternative school partnership) would have been strengthened.

The Public School System

An alternative school within the public school system faces unique problems. While it may have the support of public school administrators, an alternative is, by its very existence, a threat to the assumptions and practices which underlie traditional school organization. It is, in a sense, asking a social institution to radically alter itself. Thus covert resistance through avoidance patterns and unnecessary delay should be expected. In addition, the traditional structures of bureaucratic organization are often unable to accommodate the special needs of an alternative school. Therefore, even though the public system may support and encourage innovation, existing procedures and regulations may act to undermine innovation.

One area where the relationship with the public school system eventually raised problems was in staffing and in teacher autonomy. The teachers in the Community Free School were crucial agents in the implementation process, and the model places great emphasis on the development of positive teacher-student relationships. The student's perception of the teacher's role and of relationships among teachers and staff influences the student's own behavior. For example, students often saw teachers working late and on weekends to plan lessons, make up rosters, meet with staff members, and take students on outings. They saw teachers making a personal commitment of time and energy and also assuming a measure of responsibility for the success of the Community Free School. Teachers thereby set a model for students themselves to follow. Thus, in order to encourage students to assume responsibility for their own education, the school must be organized to give teachers extensive responsibility for their actions. It was found, moreover, that allowing teachers to follow their own routes increases their sense of competence although they may in the end accept the director's original suggestions if their own ideas do not work well.

During the implementation process, teachers depended to a great extent upon the support of those involved in the administration of the Community Free School: the project directors, the community board of directors, and the representatives of the public school system. When these participants demonstrated their support for teachers by involving themselves in the implementation process, teachers responded by assuming a great deal of responsibility for the program. Besides carrying heavy teaching loads, they worked in family group meetings and later in individual conferences with students, designed and implemented rostering procedures, communicated with parents, wrote extensive and detailed evaluations of students several times each semester, helped with administrative details, with painting and decorating the house units, and engaged in extensive team planning, teaching, and evaluation.

As the second year progressed, however, teachers began to perceive a weakening in the support of the community board and of the public school system for the program. Once they felt others were not meeting their responsibilities, teachers were then less willing to assume responsibility for this wide area of activities. It seems clear that, if a community school is to succeed and provide a viable alternative within the public system, administrative support is of primary importance in maintaining the impetus and positive attitudes of all participants in the school. When such support is not forthcoming, the burden of the implementation is shifted to those who already carry heavy commitments on their time and abilities. Inevitably, then, many necessary tasks are not carried out and many needs of the school community cannot be fulfilled.

In addition, because the success of a community school depends on a free environment with few restrictions and regulations, there is a large area of overlap between administrative and educational matters. For example, the simple issue of students smoking cigarettes in the building relates to the encouragement of a relaxed student attitude, the discipline problem of their probably sneaking a smoke if it is prohibited, and also to the fire codes which limit the extent to which this activity may be permitted. It is thus mandatory that those responsible for the educational program and those concerned with administration work in full cooperation with one another and share a common commitment to the philosophy of the school.

One of the most problematic aspects of implementing and administering the Community Free School was obtaining supplies and equipment. While the school was in the planning stages, the board of education agreed to the standard per pupil allotment of resources for the school and to the financing of the renovation of buildings and the requisition of furniture and other necessary equipment. Accordingly, a full sheaf of requisitions was filed once before the school opened and again during the subsequent summer. It was months before these undoubtedly drawn out because of administrative resistance within the board of education toward the unorthodox nature of the program and the requisitions themselves. For example, it took a year to get chairs for the houses. The principal reason for the delay was the request that the board of education order chairs of different colors, though with the same specifications as the chairs generally in use by the board at that time. In the interval resulting from these extensive delays, Community Free School funds (on loan from the university for extraordinary needs) were used to rent furniture and equipment. Expenses for such rental ran to several hundred dollars per month. By January, 1971, the Community Free School budget was depleted. While the stopgap measure of renting supplies served to provide teachers and students with the necessities for carrying on, it ultimately meant money down the drain. Naturally, all the furniture and equipment had to be returned at the end of the rental period, and no tangible assets resulted from this expense. In addition, the Community Free School budget, which had been originally intended to provide funds for development of the school above and beyond basic operating expenses, was drained by the need to pay these expenses.

Obtaining supplies and equipment was not the only drain on the budget. While the board of education had agreed to pay salaries for the fully certified teachers who worked in the school, there was no provision covering the salaries for the rest of the staff. The director was provided for by the university as were the interns from the Graduate School of Education. The funds to cover salaries for the community teachers, the community coordinator and the remaining members of the staff, then, were also drawn from the Community Free School budget. Secretarial help, also promised by the board of education, was not forthcoming for several months so that part-time help had to be hired to take care of the rapidly accumulating clerical work. Thus, the funds for development of the educational program and support of the teachers and students were largely absorbed by the costs of keeping the school in operation.

The board of education had entered into an agreement to support the Community Free School. While equipment and supplies did ultimately come through, and, while supplies such as paper and pencils were usually forthcoming via West Philadelphia High School, this support was clearly inadequate to the needs of the school in terms of facilities, equipment, transportation and staff requirements. When plans for the Community Free School were drawn up, it was evident that, while initial costs for the scattered site program would be extensive, they would be significantly less than the cost of designing, building, outfitting and staffing a new traditional school building. Once the school was running, operating costs were estimated equal to if not less than costs for operating a traditional high school of the same size. (Size based on the estimate of eventually accommodating 1000 students in five houses throughout the community).

Since staff requirements for the Community Free School differed from those of a traditional school, a system of trade-offs was proposed to provide for new positions (see pp. 34-36). It will be sufficient to note here that such a proposal would provide for full support of Community Free School staff by the board of education at no greater cost than would be necessary for a traditional high school. The board of education, however, was not agreeable to putting this system of trade-offs into operation. Money for these new positions again came out of the Community Free School development fund.

In order to move the wheels of the cumbersome bureaucratic vehicle, adequate avenues of communication must be established. The Community Free School did have formal ties with the public school system. It was operating under the jurisdiction of West Philadelphia High School, and all students in the Community Free School came from the attendance roles of this mother school. The principal of West Philadelphia High School often did not have the authority, and sometimes the willingness, to fulfill Community Free School requests and needs. Experience suggests that a public community school, rather than being attached to a mother school in the district, be directly attached to the board of education under the authority of, for instance, a deputy superintendent with sufficient power and influence to be able to expedite requests and make adjustments in the usual procedures in order to fulfill the needs of such a school.

While the Community Free School was enthusiastically endorsed by representatives of the school system, it was not possible to sustain this support consistently. Commitment to this project represented a risk to those who were also committed to the established school system. The orientation of the traditional public school administrator is toward maintaining an efficient organization. During the period of trial and error which characterized the implementation process efforts were not directed toward maximizing efficiency. Therefore to increase its efficiency and thereby its effectiveness, public school administrators involved with the school began to fall back into traditional patterns of thought and action. This tendency raises serious questions: Is it possible to implement such a community free school within the public educational system? Are the goals of public education aimed at making the system efficient, at the expense of the people it serves? Of course, it takes time to establish a working relationship between a new school and a traditional board of education. During this time, some compromises and accommodations will have to be made on both sides. Yet the success of any public community free school ultimately depends on the ability of the public school system to respond to the needs of the communities it serves. If this response is not ultimately forthcoming, then the system itself will have to be changed.

THE SCHOOL COMMUNITY

The structure and philosophy of the Community Free School model posits for students an important and vital role in making decisions about their own education as well as about the operation and direction of their school. It requires commitment and action on their part, not only in terms of their own educational goals, but also in terms of the welfare of fellow students and the entire school community. Indeed, one of the important goals of the school model is the development of a sense of responsibility for the success of others. To ensure that students would become actively involved in the decision-making process and would begin to accept responsibility for policy making and development, formal mechanisms were set up: a steering committee and a judicial board. The former was to deal in general with policy decisions that affected the entire student body, e.g., curriculum, environment, evaluation. The judicial board had the responsibility to make decisions in cases where the actions of a particular student or group of students were detrimental to the student body and/or the entire school community, e.g., extreme class cutting, stealing, etc.

A further aim of these two bodies was to ease the transition of all students from a highly traditional educational setting to a more free and open one where student input was respected and desired. The intent was to put students in a position where they could assume responsibility and take action. These two groups were organized soon after the opening of the school, and at one time or another each house had its own steering committee and judicial board. Representatives to these groups were elected by each family group, and each also included a teacher representative.

The success of these two student bodies varied from house to house and from committee to committee. In one house, the steering committee was able to gather more than 30% of the students to meet with the entire faculty to discuss their concerns about teachers' attitudes and curriculum content. Not only was there a lively discussion and debate, but three specific proposals were adopted to deal with problems. In addition, both students and teachers agreed to make this type of discussion a weekly happening. These formal student organizations enjoyed periods of relative success and accomplishment, and in general it was found that, while they could work well in a given, specifically defined situation, they were not feasible as permanent mechanisms.

During the second semester of the school's operation both groups began to take less and less responsibility for decision-making and for dealing with actions of fellow students. There were a variety of reasons for this development:

1. In some cases, students were reluctant to make decisions regarding disciplinary action involving fellow students. One house, for instance, found itself unable to deal with a serious case of stealing for this reason. All houses experienced problems with gangs and fear of retaliation by gang members prevented judicial boards from taking disciplinary action against these students.

2. Students found themselves unable to make serious policy decisions, and the steering committee began to look more and more like the typical high school student council, dealing mostly with social activities such as dances and picnics.

3. While student members of the steering committee were required to report to their family groups after each meeting, they did not always do so.

4. Finally, the mechanism of such formal organizations requires the same group of people to make policy and decisions throughout the school year. This was found to be unnecessary in a school of this size which is based on an open and participatory philosophy.

In fact, it was found that an informal, town-meeting type of organization was the most useful and most acceptable way of making decisions and dealing with problems. Small ad hoc committees were formed from general meetings to deal with specific issues. These groups then dissolved after performing their function. The composition of such groups depended on the particular issue involved. If it was a question of a school dance, certain students might be involved; on a question of curriculum, other students and more teachers would participate.

Aside from the town-meeting type of organization, it was also found that students tended to handle serious situations themselves without the need for formal bodies and procedures. Not only did students as a group tend to deal with such problems informally, but even on an individual basis, they dealt directly with issues that were of concern to them. One boy, a former gang member, described his experience in the Community Free School.

"At West I was always getting into rock fights and fights with teachers. Here I get along with everybody. . . At West there were too many people. Now I can sit down and talk about special things. Some people I talk with about books, other about what I did over the weekend. I talk to teachers all the time about what I want to do, what I think we should do in class, what I dislike about what we do in class. We have a period you come in and just rap to teachers."

Thus, the small, personal and informal atmosphere of the Community Free School made unnecessary in many cases the organization of formal mechanisms to deal with problems and policy. It was just as well, even better sometimes, to allow the informality of student and student-teacher relationships to resolve important issues. In some cases, more explicit procedures were required, but these were better developed in ad hoc committees which dealt with specific issues rather than by the development of permanent and perhaps rigid structures. Moreover, one can indeed discern students' acceptance of their new responsible role in the ways they naturally dealt with situations that arose and were potentially problematic.

Professional Teaching Staff

As teachers responded to their new roles within the Community Free School, new expectations also emerged. Teaching in an experimental atmosphere requires total commitment and great energy, imagination and humanness. In order to be truly effective, teachers must feel that their input and their decisions bear a direct relationship to the school's implementation and successful operation. The teacher who feels that what he says and does makes a significant difference not only in the classroom but in all matters relating to the life of the school will be more willing to commit the enormous time and energy necessary for its success. If the intended level of teachers' freedom, responsibility and control is not maintained, if teachers are beset by feelings of frustration and helplessness, if they feel that what they do and say no longer makes a difference, one can only expect a retreat into the traditional classroom and the traditional public school structure.

There came a time in the operation of the Community Free School when teachers had reached a significant level of commitment to the school, to parents, and to students. They felt at the same time, however, that their own commitment was not matched by a real acknowledgment on the part of the community board of the importance of teachers' feelings and opinions in the operation of the school. Thus, they requested voting representation on the community board. The following chronology of events involved in this request demonstrates the very real possibility for teachers' accepting the new role posited by the Community Free School model and the power of this role for creating commitment and concern.

March, 1970: Initially, there was indeed a sense of community and common purpose. Teachers' field notes from this period indicate their personal commitment to the project's success and their gratification at being able to work with the community on an equal basis. Moreover, in the beginning there was relatively frequent interaction among teachers and the community board: board members observed the operation of the school, talked with teachers informally, and met with them on a formal basis to choose new staff members.

May, 1970: Later, however, when certain elements of the implementation became problematic, such as the question of free time, teachers sensed a growing distance between themselves and the board. They wanted the board to take effective action to solve this problem and sensed a lack of leadership from the community board. When the board failed to act to help them solve the free time issue, teachers questioned the role of the board in relation to themselves and in relation to the operation of the school. When board members became less and less visible in the daily operation of the school, teachers felt they were not being taken seriously by the community and that the board's interest was of a kind and degree different from their own commitment.

September, 1970: At this point, when the problems of the previous spring had still not been dealt with, teachers reiterated in their field notes their uncertainty about the commitment of the community board and their own relationship to the community board. They felt that the teachers' and community board's philosophies of the school were different, that the board was not "with them." They were not certain as to how available the board would be as a resource for teachers or as to the board's expectations of teachers. One teacher felt insecurity on the part of the board regarding drastic educational changes and experimental methods and goals.

October, 1970: The teachers presented a petition to the community board asking for representation on the board by teachers, students, and parents. The board denied this request, claiming that the control of the school was theirs and that the relationship between them and the teachers was a traditional one of management and labor, i.e., the teachers worked for the community and were thus subject to decisions made by the community board alone. The chairman later stated that the board would not change its decision, that board members felt the teachers were interested in developing their own school "not our school. We don't want your thing really."

These events suggest a traditional management vs. labor explanation, but this is only a surface description of more fundamental differences. The community board perceived as its own activity the operation of a school which they could control. Control of the school was, furthermore, a manifestation of minority group identity. Teachers' requests for representation and for help from the community board were perceived by this board as threats to their role and responsibilities.

The community board dealt with this threat to identify by the only means possible: they refused the teachers representation on the board. This decision, which came at the end of the series of events described above, effectively restricted the area between the two groups where cooperation and compromise were possible.

The fundamental nature of this issue in the implementation of alternative schools becomes even more striking when one compares the interaction between teachers and community board in the spring of 1970 with the interaction that took place the following fall. In the beginning of the school's operation, the strategic and tactical issues of acquiring facilities, equipment, and materials made the operation of the school the primary concern of all participants — thus supporting the community board's notion of its own role. Moreover, the occasions of cooperative interaction between the board and teachers were not perceived as threats; teachers assumed they had a say in decision-making but did not test this power because there was no need to do so until differences were clearly apparent. Only when differences became evident and explicit could definitions of roles and spheres of action actually surface above the assumed bases of interaction.

While the attempt by teachers to assume a voting and decision-making role on the community board failed, the events related above illustrate the very real potential of a school, based on and implemented by a participatory philosophy, to create and sustain a new kind of role and commitment for public school teachers. While limited by the community board's denial of voting membership, the teachers had, nevertheless, accepted the responsibilities called for and performed them well.

Although the student body was 98% black, and all the community teachers were black, the professional teaching staff was predominately white (4 black and 16 white teachers). As a result, the question of white teachers teaching black students was an issue that all participants in the Community Free School project faced. The community board made a concentrated effort during the summer of 1970 to attract more qualified black public high school teachers to apply for the new positions created when the school expanded to three houses. They failed, however, for several reasons:

1. An agreement with the board of education required that teachers in the Community Free School come originally from the mother school, West Philadelphia High School, which itself had a limited number of black teachers. There was some lip service paid to the idea of trying to attract teachers from other districts within the city. However, because of administrative red tape, this kind of recruiting never took place.

2. Those black teachers who were at West Philadelphia High School felt that to go to a small, alternative school would be "letting down" the majority of students who would remain in the main building. "Experiments come and go" was the general feeling among these teachers; they felt that there is a tendency to get excited about an alternative school and, at the same time, to forget about the students who are not a part of the innovative project.

3. Some black teachers feared that, if the experiment failed, they would not be able to get their jobs back, that they would be transferred to another school and be taken advantage of.

The general feeling among community board members was that a sensitive adaptable, honest and knowledgeable person was needed to teach. If he/she were black, all the better. But a competent white teacher (as defined by the community board) was more desirable in the

Community Free School than a less competent black teacher. This attitude was also shared, to a large extent, by the students in the Community Free School.

Another group of professional teachers that held a vital position on the Community Free School staff was the graduate interns. These interns were students working toward their masters degree in education at the University of Pennsylvania. Theirs was a volunteer position called for in the model, as a way of lowering the student-teacher ratio without additional expenditure of funds.

The interns worked with the certified teachers of the staff as members of teaching teams. Full teaching responsibility was granted to the interns, and no distinctions in status were made between certified teachers and interns, all were teachers despite their titles. The entire staff had to work together as a cohesive unit if the Community Free School was to be a success.

The interns received close supervision, which legitimized in the eyes of the community their contributions and responsibilities. Video-tapings and weekly critique sessions with the educational consultant were also used to increase and enhance their teaching ability.

The Community Free School benefitted in that it was able to lower its student-teacher ratio without expenditure of funds, while the university was presented with an opportunity for offering more comprehensive and satisfying field experience.

Many benefits were garnered by the interns themselves who were faced with a "real-life" teaching situation and who were given real responsibility within this position. They gained experience in all facets of implementing and running a school and in meeting the problems involved in such an undertaking. Moreover, they were able to increase their teaching abilities through their close contact with the educational consultant, experienced classroom teachers, and the use of the videotapes of their own teaching.

A major portion of the success of the Community Free School depended upon the teacher's willingness to respond when they were given responsibility. The graduate interns were always among the first to take such responsibility, and were among the most cooperative, innovative members of the school. Their abilities and dedication were recognized by both the certified teaching staff and the students. As a measure of their success, when all of the graduate interns applied for positions as certified teachers at the end of the first semester, their requests were unanimously supported by the remaining staff, and 60% of the student body signed a petition for their appointments.

Community Teachers

During the first year of operation two community teachers were selected by the community board to work at the Community Free School. During the second year, the number of community teachers grew to five. Community teachers worked part time at the Community Free School and were on salary. It was therefore essential that their involvement be meaningful and that they become a real asset to the program in order to justify the commitment of resources. Several problems did emerge, however, which might be avoided in the future with better planning and organization of this aspect of the program.

The community teachers came from a variety of backgrounds: several were parents with children in high school or approaching high school age; one community teacher had children in the Community Free School; a few were young community residents. They differed in levels of education and in the extent of their experience. None had had previous experience with community schools, and few had had previous contact with high school teaching.

In order to familiarize community teachers with the goals of the school and with teaching techniques, a training program would be necessary. However, community teachers joined the program just as the school opened and were, therefore, unable to participate in the orientation session for teachers. As a result, during the first semester a gap existed between full time teachers and community teachers. A problem also existed in that the community teachers often felt inferior to the regular teachers and were unused to being considered the equal of a teacher. The teachers occasionally forgot this as well, and this sometimes resulted in the ineffective use of the community teachers.

Nevertheless, community teachers made substantial contributions by drawing on their special skills in working with individual students or small groups of students and by developing good relationships with students in general.

Two instances in particular are worthy of mention. One young community teacher, himself a writer and poet, conducted a writing workshop which became a great success and was especially liked by students. At the end of the term, students themselves produced a magazine of their own poetry, essays, fiction, and art work as a result of this workshop. Another community teacher was an accomplished amateur musician. When the Community Free School was given a piano, she began giving music lessons, classes in music theory, and even established a student chorus.

Even those community teachers who did not possess such special talents were able to contribute to the program by aiding students in the math workshop and the reading workshop, by organizing various activities, and by acting, in part, as liaisons between community residents and the school itself. Indeed, community teachers were very successful in gathering parent support and participation: contacting parents, organizing meetings, and explaining the Community Free School program. Clearly, the best utilization of this valuable community resource lies in expanding the involvement and responsibility of community teachers, defining a common ground which community teachers and full time teachers can share, and continuing to draw on the specific skills and abilities of the community teachers. The reason this did not happen to its fullest extent is principally due to the lack of a sufficient training program for community teachers and the inexperience of the professional teaching staff in utilizing paraprofessional support. They must be selected at the same time as the regular teachers and participate in all training activities. By sharing initial experiences with other teachers and working together with them from the start, community teachers can indeed fill the role defined by the PASS Model.

Parents

Perhaps the most difficult kind of involvement in the Community Free School to encourage and sustain is that of community parents. Most parents have accepted the traditional passive role in relation to the public schools their children attend. Naturally, they want the best possible school for their children, but they have never been offered the opportunity to participate in developing such a school; if they were asked, many of them would not feel qualified to contribute. As a result, many parents attend PTA functions and other gatherings simply to hear reports from teachers and to discuss particular problems their sons and daughters may be having.

At the Community Free School, parents were invited and expected to involve themselves in their children's education. First, they were asked to decide whether their children, once selected by random sample, would attend the new school or remain at West Philadelphia High School. Parents were sent information on the school and were contacted by community board members and staff in order to be informed of the goals and program of the new school.

Shortly after the opening of the school, house parents met on several occasions. Proposals discussed included keeping the school open in the evening and on weekends while staffed by parent volunteers and planning for informal gatherings of parents to discuss the progress of the school, to answer questions and to make suggestions. The hope was also that some parents might participate in the various educational programs rather than simply "staff" the school when needed. Meetings, however, were erratic and concrete projects did not develop.

The following year, parents in one of the house units formed the Very Involved Parents (VIPS) and met monthly to plan a car pool, a lunch program, an arts and crafts program, donations of equipment, and other projects. Parents also expressed a desire to be represented at community board meetings. The lunch program was set up and ran for several months with great success; rugs and furniture were acquired as donations, and vending machines were placed in the house. Other projects were not so successful. Finally, teachers and students in the houses called periodic open house meetings in which parents, students and teachers met in the evening to discuss the progress of the program and individual student progress.

Despite several attempts, however, parents involvement remained limited, and the number of parents active in the school was small, although proportionally greater than the parent participation usually found in the traditional high school. Many did not have the time to become involved even on a part time volunteer basis; others did not have transportation facilities to get to the house unit. In addition, many were as wary as their children of the new school. Yet, the PASS Model calls for parent involvement to the extent that they share in the decision-making process and operation of the school. While all community residents have a natural and vested interest in the success of a community school, parents would seem to have the most immediate and important stake in it. It seems probable that, if the community representatives to the community board were parents of children in the school, this would assure their sustained and active involvement.

As already seen, most of the community members of the board felt their work in the daily operation of the school was complete when the school had been established. Had most of these members been parents of children attending the Community Free School, their interest in all aspects of the program and in all participants in the program would certainly have continued. It may well be that for future implementations of the PASS Model, board members should be chosen from the ranks of those people who have children in the school itself.

There are other ways in which parents may become active and involved in a community free school. Mothers who do not have other jobs may want to become outside instructors and teach what they can best offer; those who would like a part time job may apply to become community teachers; others who have the time and can volunteer their services may do secretarial work in the house units. They may work with individual or small groups of students in remedial programs or even teach in a workshop. Parents may make many kinds of contributions to a community school depending on the economic level of the community.

That the plan to involve parents did meet with some success is evidenced by their growing acceptance of the program, their positive reactions to student evaluations, and by several enthusiastic endorsements of the school. These indicated that parents had begun to overcome their traditional hesitation. Alternative schools need to develop means whereby parents can contribute in many ways, working on short-term projects and maintaining close contact with the staff and students in developing the program.

THE EDUCATIONAL PROGRAM

Inside Program

The following section explains and illustrates some of the important aspects of the curriculum of the in-house educational

85

program of the Community Free School. The content and process of developing curriculum should, of course, reflect and be based on the total educational philosophy of the school. Curriculum, no matter how well designed and implemented, cannot by itself ensure that learning will take place. The school environment has a far greater potential to affect, positively or negatively, the value of the curriculum. The educational environment must be supportive of and conducive to learning experiences. Given the importance of developing curriculum, several crucial processes were built into its development in the Community Free School.

1. Students must have concrete evidence that they are learning something. This requires a constant flow of information and feedback between teachers and students. This was provided for in informal ways in the Community Free School, by the easy interaction between students and teachers. In some cases, it was necessary to provide students with traditional methods and materials like textbooks to give them this sense of learning something and to provide them with familiar aspects of the educational process so as to ease their transition into a different kind of learning.

2. Student input into curriculum development must be sought by teachers and staff. Thus, teachers were constantly available to students to discuss class activities as well as individual concerns. Teachers' meetings were open to students, and their suggestions and evaluations were readily listened to. Joint decisions on curriculum content and methods were often made by students and teachers, and, in some cases, teachers sought student opinion by formal evaluative means, i.e., written statements and questionnaires.

3. Since the prime purpose of the Community Free School was to meet the needs, interests, and abilities of students, the content and methods of the inside program were constantly changing and open to change. Sometimes these changes were made to meet the needs of a particular student; at other times they were made in accordance with the wishes of an entire group. Furthermore, complete re-rostering took place several times during the school year in an effort to respond to students' needs and interests.

4. Action learning methods were built into the educational program as much as possible to give students the opportunity to learn from

doing. Thus, research projects involving investigation of the environment and local resources were often included in the program; improvisational and simulation techniques were used in the classroom; students were encouraged to help each other and thus learn by teaching as well as developing a sense of responsibility for fellow students.

This section illustrates three forms that curriculum development took in the Community Free School. All share the basic goals of making students responsible for their own learning, individualizing instruction, and developing a sense of responsibility for the welfare of others. The minicourses, the reading and writing workshops, and the math labs were all integral parts of the daily program of the Community Free School. The January program developed by teachers and students together was an experiment in the use of different topics for and different methods of learning-teaching.

Minicourses

A nongraded, alternative school which aims to individualize each student's learning experiences requires its teachers to be flexible, imaginative and extremely resourceful. Given a heterogeneous student body, a scarcity of books and materials, Community Free School teachers began to write much of their own curriculum. They found that by creating minicourses — short, complete units of study focused on a central concept or theme, e.g., Teaching History through Music — they were best able to individualize learning experiences and attend to the students' varying skill and interest levels.

In writing these miniunits teachers found that one of the most difficult tasks was to provide sufficient material to meet the needs of the heterogeneously grouped students. In several classes teachers found that since reading ability varied widely, they required either several different sets of material or one set aimed at the average skill level. This problem led teachers to include several alternative procedures and resource materials within each of the units to meet the needs of small groups with different ability levels.

Heterogeneously grouped students present a great challenge to the teacher. While there are many problems with this kind of grouping, there also exists a tremendous potential for learning, especially if students can be motivated to help each other learn. It is no secret to anyone that one of the most effective ways to learn is to teach. Having students of different interests and skill levels in the same group offers this possibility.

It has been stated several times that students were not used to the varied learning opportunities which existed at the Community Free School. (The need to see visible proof of learning and accomplishment was widely felt among students.) The more traditional method of using a routine format, frequent quizzes, and standardized tests was not followed in the Community Free School. The break with traditional teaching/learning methods produced a high level of uncertainty and insecurity in many students who felt they were not learning anything. Students felt, for example, that discussing the Black Panthers and their role in creating social change in America was "fun" and "interesting," but it wasn't "learning." This complaint from students led teachers to devise in their minicourse units series of exercises which provided immediate and evaluative feedback to students. These exercises demonstrated to the student that something real had transpired and that he was actually learning. By saving these assignments in the student's folders, it was also possible to go back to the beginning of a unit with him and measure his progress and point out his problem areas. Because the units were relatively short (four to six weeks), students could review their thought processes during the course of a unit and sense that real learning had taken place.

In addition to providing concrete learning activities which actively involved the student, successful minicourses were well structured and gave the student a sense of continuity and of orderly progression from one concept to another and from one activity to another. A good example of this aspect of the minicourses is a chart developed by a group of teachers and included in one of their units. On the chart, students recorded information learned in class. "Student response to this procedure was one of the most positive results of the class," the teachers wrote. It gave the students a sense of the overall structure and direction of the unit.

The minicourses* used during the first year of the Community Free School's operation were not predesigned. That is, they were

---

*It is outside the scope of this book to include the units here, but some of the minicourse units are available from the authors.

literally developed by teachers on the spot who planned and created a few lessons at a time. At a later date, with the aid of a research and development grant, the authors and several teachers worked these units into a systematic format. It was found, in the final preparation of these units, that, if a predesigned curriculum unit, the primary focus of which is specifically designed activities, is to be of any real help to a teacher, it must include an overall rationale. Such a rationale would contain the following information: First, an introduction to the unit, with an explanation of the relationship of activities to one another, and concrete methods for encouraging student awareness of the structure and sequence of the unit activities as a whole. Second, special emphasis to key activities in each unit, so that the teacher can be flexible in dropping or reversing the order of activities without reducing the effectiveness of the unit in meeting its primary objectives. Alternative suggestions for implementing these key activities should also be included, either in the introductory section or in the instructions for that particular activity. Third, it should specify the background required of a teacher using the particular unit, and whether the unit will be most effective in a team-taught or individually-taught classroom. Again, alternative suggestions should be included to enable the individual teacher or the teacher team to use the unit as effectively as possible in the particular classroom situation.

One last point should be made regarding predesigned units. Most minicourses were team planned and team taught, as were most of the teaching/learning activities in the Community Free School. It was assumed that these units would be applicable to single-teacher classrooms and that the individual teacher would have sufficient background to deal with the subject matter involved. It was discovered in subsequent teachings of these units, however, that a predesigned curriculum unit cannot in itself supply the teacher with all the background knowledge he needs. A short summary and bibliography can be included, but the teacher must be familiar with the field covered by the unit. Given a sufficient range and variety of curriculum minilessons, any teacher should be able to select a unit which he feels confident to teach.

Reading and Writing Workshops

Because basic skills in reading and writing were the most problematic area for many Community Free School students, it was decided that special attention would be devoted to the development of these skills in a special workshop as well as in subject-matter courses. Each house, therefore, set up its own workshop which served also as a general library for the entire house. Each student spent at least two hours per week in the workshop during which he individually or in small groups worked on his skills that needed improvement. Each student's work, including initial reading test scores, was kept in a file in the workshop so that his progress could be recorded and seen by him.

While the reading and writing workshops took different forms in each house, their basic aim was the same: to improve the reading and writing skills of the students. A description of the structure and content of the workshop in one of the houses illustrates the variety of skill building activities available to students. The workshop in the house under discussion was structured to allow for maximum choice for the students from among various activities planned and designed by teachers. Each week the students were given a short "browsing" period during which they chose their project for the day. Each student made a journal-like entry in his folder at the end of each session, telling what he had done that day in the workshop. Tape recorders, typewriters, and other equipment were available to allow students to work individually or in small groups.

The teachers themselves were responsible for developing at least one activity a week. Every two weeks, the humanities teachers from all the houses met to exchange materials, ideas, and to discuss problems and their solutions.

There was a wide variety of materials available for reading practice including, for example, the New York Times, local Philadelphia newspapers, short story collections, fictional and nonfictional works, and popular and literary magazines. "Just reading in a corner" was considered as valuable an activity as directed reading exercises. Games like Scrabble, Scribbage, and Probe were used to build spelling and vocabulary skills. Teachers developed crossword puzzles and sentence building exercises for use by individual students. Programmed texts and Educational Testing Service preparatory material were also available for students if they needed these kinds of exercises. Teachers also developed a variety of exercises, themes and materials for the improvement of writing skills. In some cases, students kept a personal journal as a way of practicing writing skills.

Student response to the reading and writing workshops differed from house to house. One unit found that attendance was not as high as in classes, for students found the workshop too unstructured. But for the most part, the students felt it a welcome change from the other classes and attended regularly. One house found that many students who were not rostered into a particular workshop period came in anyway during their free time period. Another house started off with group work and then became more individual as students got used to the unstructured program. Students seemed to like the programmed materials, particularly for specific reading problems, and, in general, they tended to be willing to write more.

Math Labs

Another similar workshop structure called math labs was set up for the math program. Again, work was individualized and student progress was recorded in individual folders. Students worked at their own pace, using textbooks when appropriate, exercises developed by teachers, and gaming techniques. Students worked on basic math skills, algebra, geometry, elementary functions, and basic mathematical concepts. The goals of the math labs were, of course, to improve basic math skills as well as to prepare students for college entrance exams and college courses. Perhaps more importantly, the aim was also to give students an appreciation and understanding of numbers and of the ways in which math is used in daily life and is related to their own lives.

While students responded enthusiastically to and worked hard in both the reading and writing workshop and the math labs, these two aspects of the inside program were not without their problems. Teachers, for instance, sometimes found it difficult to give substantial attention to each student during these periods although there were at least two and sometimes more teachers in each session. One initial difficulty was that students had had very little experience with reading and had never done much writing. One teacher wrote about her experiences in dealing with this problem:

> . . . I asked them all to write about their feelings or experiences of the day before. It was really hard for a lot of them. They didn't know what to write. They couldn't write. They didn't want to write and it's significant to me, having taught kids before who didn't have this problem, to really note the difficulty they have. So I'm going to have them write every day

and set aside a special time because only then can the kids really start getting into some writing.

It is significant, in the light of this early comment, that by the end of the semester teachers noted that students were "doing an overwhelming amount of writing" and were *willing* to write.

The math labs also experienced some problems, particularly in trying to show students the need for and importance of math in their own lives. Even the use of a computer terminal and math games were not enough to make math enjoyable to some students, although the majority were "turned on" to math by these techniques. One of the most significant outcomes of the math labs came in terms of the goals of the Community Free School, a willingness to take responsibility for the welfare of others. One math teacher recorded the following comments in his field notes:

> In the beginning, I found almost no students willing either to help or be helped by others in many of the classes. I think there has been a noticeable change in this respect. The students who have moved faster are usually very willing to help explain problems, and more students seem amenable to peer help. I don't think this happened very frequently in these students' past experience.

Special Programs

As the confusion created by the delays in renovating facilities began to subside during Phase III (the fall of 1970), teachers and students began to explore some of the possibilities available to them by creating their own inside program. In an attempt to reach more students and to diversify the curriculum, two of the three houses set up special four-week programs which were dramatically different from the programs that had been conducted to that point.

The following is the rationale offered by one staff member for embarking on this ambitious restructuring:

> The teachers are interested in finding a way to work more closely with each other and, to some extent, trying something

experimental; and, there is an interest in providing kids with a learning experience that brings into sharp relief the role of responsibility within the context of the Community Free School.

Towards the end of Phase III, with this as their aim, teachers, students and staff worked out the details of an experimental inter-disciplinary program to be run in the afternoons for the month of January. The regular inside course program was to be condensed into the morning hours.

The following objectives were listed by one house as the goals of their January program:

1. To help students experience a process by moving from an idea to a product;

2. To develop the ability to explain a process verbally;

3. To develop appreciation for the work of other people;

4. To produce at least one product that the student would want to talk about or show;

5. To have the student understand how he participated in interdisciplinary learning;

6. To be responsive to the working needs of others;

7. To have teachers of different disciplines working together;

8. To create an atmosphere in which teachers can explore unfamiliar ways of teaching and planning;

9. To have teachers accept the validity of nonverbal activity.

A list of courses offered during this period follows:

1. The Role of Women: A course about the position of women in today's society. Their jobs, their real differences with men, equality, their role with children, their psychology.

2. Introduction to Jazz: In this course we will listen to jazz, visit radio stations that play jazz, have guest speakers. Active participation is required.

3. Ways of Knowing: A look at the occult. The world of the supernatural — does it really exist? We will study astrology, reincarnation, the claims of communication with the dead, ESP , and more.

4. Flatland: What happens in a two-dimensional world? Take this course to find out. Use your knowledge of math to analyze politics. Students must have taken or be taking geometry.

5. Animated Film-making with Geometric Forms: Making films with moving abstract shapes. Experiment freely with shape, sound, and color.

6. Dome Building: Plan and construct your own living structure and environment.

7. Psychocybernetics: The dynamics of personality — yours and others'.

8. Sex Education: You know what this is about.

9. Films and Nonverbal Responses: See some movies and express your reactions to them without using words.

10. Balloon Sculptures: A new way of making sculptures. Come and see how.

11. Knitting and Weaving and Crocheting:

12. Dramatics:

13. Murals: Make something really impressive on the wall.

It should be remembered that this attempt at remodeling the curriculum was originated and implemented by the teachers and students. It was planned on Saturdays and evenings and was the result of a felt need on the part of both groups. It is significant that the environment of the Community Free School permitted this kind of freedom and change, the development and use of a variety of means to meet the objectives of the school.

The Outside Program

In February, 1970, when the school opened, students were given a colorful catalogue describing the 50 offerings of the outside program. This was expanded to 90 in the second semester. This was quite a switch for students who were used to traditional courses in a traditional environment. They were accustomed to a limited number of options and expected school activities to be limited to the school building if not the four walls of the classroom. Not only had students never seen such a wide range of course offerings, but they were unable to relate these kinds of courses to their previous academic or educational experiences, new courses such as the World of Construction, Physical Therapy, and Animated Film-making. Many thought the program was simply a short afternoon session or a supplement to the inside program. Because students had never been involved in such a situation before, the program at first meant little to them even though the catalogue described the course offerings in detail and even though a job fair was organized to explain these outside courses to them. It is understandable, then, that problems arose in the implementation of this aspect of the Community Free School program.

Because of limited opportunity and the network of exclusive gang turfs superimposed on West Philadelphia neighborhoods, many students had never traveled freely within or outside the community. Consequently, parts of the community outside their own small neighborhoods or streets were unfamiliar to them; students had no conception of what lay behind the doors of most local businesses and other institutional buildings. A major goal of the outside program was, therefore, to expose students to this "outside world," to allow them to see the kinds of opportunities which exist in their community, the qualifications needed to benefit from these opportunities, and the relevance of their academic studies to the "real world of work." Once the program was underway and students had attended their first classes in the community, the geographic distance between students and outside instructors had been bridged; however, the social distance between them would take much longer to disappear. Some students were wary of these new environments and hesitant to involve themselves. In one class, for example, the instructor noted that a student looked ill. When she asked what the problem was, the girl replied sheepishly, asking to go to the bathroom. The student felt that not knowing where the bathroom was was a sign of ignorance, and she would rather have been sick than appear stupid!

Outside course instructors were just as new to the experience as the students. Their confusion and surprise were evident in a questionnaire distributed by the community coordinator's office soon after the program began. In their responses, half of the instructors noted that they had expected students to be less motivated and less able to grasp subject matter than they subsequently found them to be; the other half expected more motivation and more understanding on the part of students. This confusion became apparent during observations made of the community classes. Although many of the teachers were enthusiastic and willing, most had never taught before; those few with teaching experience were not used to working with inner-city high school students. For the most part, these instructors had attended traditional high schools, and their only exposure to teaching methods was based on the rigid, traditional model by which they themselves had been taught. This structured approach usually calls for a lecture or a question-and-answer format.

The following is an illustration of this problem, taken from a staff member's report of an elective course at a local bank:

> The course started out with six or seven students; shortly only one was left. I went to see the instructor to find out why. He is very nice, means well, likes the student, but is boring her (and me) terribly. He just lectures for two hours, doesn't let the student answer questions he asks but answers them himself. The student's part is completely passive.

This illustration also points up the very great need for a training program for instructors of outside elective courses. Although the staff members did meet with these outside instructors several times to discuss problems and make suggestions for improvement, lack of time and sufficient personnel made continuing training sessions infeasible.

Despite these problems, however, enough of the outside courses were successful to warrant continuation and expansion of the program as the school itself expanded. Two courses which did succeed and were very popular with students are described below. One of the most successful courses was given at a local bank under the title Personal Money Management. The instructor planned a number of different activities with the students. She included experts from various bank departments in each of her lessons. The course outline included learning how to open a checking or savings account, the subtleties of installment credit, how to recognize consumer fraud, and how to buy insurance. She used guest speakers, films and simulated case studies to get her points across. Student response was enthusiastic: they participated actively and found people at the bank to be friendly and interested in their lives.

In the course on The World of Construction, six students were picked up and driven every Wednesday afternoon to an actual job site. They were met by a project foreman who introduced them to the many aspects of the construction business. Students had the opportunity to read blueprints, work with surveyors, and question everyone including architects and engineers. According to one construction executive, "The course gave the students real insight into the working of the construction company, kept their interest at a high level, helped company personnel, even helped improve communication between job personnel and students. The course was an instrument for involving six students in a meaningful educational experience as well as opening up possible employment opportunities for these minority students."

In addition to the problem of unrealistic expectations, which led to high absentee rates and in some cases to the cancellation of outside courses, a serious logistical problem emerged in the outside program. The PASS Model calls for the use of a minibus moving constantly throughout the community, taking students to and from courses, and enabling the school to operate on a flexible, modular, and individualized schedule. A minibus, or for that matter, any bus was impossible to come by. The board of education could provide only one bus for four hours a day, and that service required an enormous amount of red tape. When this bus was used, it arrived irregularly, thus forcing students to use public transportation at great expense to the school and with great waste of time. Often students were late to their outside courses or to their in-house classes as a result of the lack of efficient transportation. This situation led many instructors to feel that students were irresponsible and uninterested in their courses.

One remedy for this problem of transportation was in the hiring of a University of Pennsylvania bus to serve in place of the school district bus. Although this solved the problem of transporting students promptly from house to businesses and institutions, it proved too costly to continue on a permanent basis. Thus, a bus or minibus provided by the school board to be used exclusively by the Community Free School units seem essential to the efficient operation of the outside program.

Yet, because the program succeeded as well as it did under the most trying of circumstances and because the outside instructors were most willing and interested in the program, it should be possible to design an outside program which will indeed come close to meeting the objectives outlined in the PASS Model. What follows is a series of "ground rules," consisting of guidelines and recommendations for establishing an effective program of this kind.

In order for members of the business community to interact effectively with a community school, new administrative structures must be established to insure that the outside program is properly organized, scheduling is accurate, and outside instructors receive the training and ongoing support they need. The community coordinator must understand fully the goals and objectives of the school and of the outside program. He should possess the experience and expertise to deal with executives, managers of business and industry, and others who are to be the teachers. He should also have knowledge of and experience with teaching-learning theories and methods and be able to relate well to students and teachers.

While the community coordinator bears the main responsibility for the operation of the outside program, he cannot carry out this responsibility alone. Businessmen and their companies must commit themselves at the executive level to genuine involvement with such a program. First, through participating in a business advisory board, business leaders can assist the community coordinator in administering and expanding the program. Secondly, by allowing their employees the time to plan and evaluate their courses, they will be giving the support an instructor needs to be an effective teacher. Instructors may use this time to plan and evaluate curriculum, attend training workshops, and discuss problems and experiences with other instructors and with in-house teachers.

The professional teachers can in fact provide a great deal of assistance to the community coordinator as well as to the outside instructors. The community coordinator's office may arrange times when it is possible for teachers to meet with the outside instructors, help them construct lesson plans and work out the best methods of relaying their knowledge to the students. Moreover, since each house is small and each student has a family group teacher who follows his progress in all areas of school life, special problems which arise can be dealt with in a personal and individual way. The teacher from business is not expected to go it alone; rather, one of the goals of involving the business community is to encourage a cooperative effort of all community members in the educational process.

From the Community Free School experience it appears that outside instructors felt least secure in dealing with students and trying to teach in new and unfamiliar ways. It seems clear that those involved in the program should draw on their strengths to gain confidence and provide for a more meaningful course offering. Participants from the business community should, therefore, be encouraged to teach what they know best, to base the learning experience on their own areas of expertise. The general criteria used in selecting a teacher should be knowledge of the subject area and the ability to convey this knowledge. Men and women in business or who work in institutional settings are faced with the same problems that face professional teachers: how to keep the students involved and interested, how to ask the right questions, how to judge when learning is taking place. Consequently, a teacher who is familiar and comfortable with the subject matter, who knows what materials are available and what is going on in his field will be able to concentrate on the always more difficult task of getting information across.

Another important ground rule is to structure the outside program to be consistent with the overall objectives of the community school model. A staff member's report from the fall of 1970 notes:

> Successful [outside] courses have two factors in common. First, and perhaps most important, the instructors have good

rapport with the students. They know them by name, are interested in their lives outside the course . . . and know how to work with them. The other necessary ingredient is to have a course in which there is real student participation. When the students are actively involved in learning, physically involved even, they enjoy it more, are more interested, and thus learn more. . . .

Thus, courses should be developed which encourage active participation by the students and individualized or small group instruction. Courses should be generally limited to a maximum of twelve students, and lecturing and other passive teaching methods should be discouraged. The aim is for students to become involved in the program: to handle the duties of a loan officer in a bank, conduct tests in a hospital or company laboratory, sell insurance, and participate in any other active means of learning. In a course conducted by the Veterans Administration Hospital, for instance, students actually worked with patients in therapy. Whenever possible the student should have the opportunity to involve himself in the actual work experience and even assume some responsibility in the business or institution where the experience takes place.

One of the problems which has plagued the outside program has been the lack of sufficient and trained staff in the office of the community coordinator to conduct an adequate teacher training program and to follow up preservice training with periodic visits to the classroom. A systematic and organized teacher training program for these outside instructors must be established. The training program should involve a pretraining period with ongoing and follow-up evaluation. It should help the instructor understand the kinds of students with whom he will be dealing and the overall educational model of the school. Instructors in the outside courses should learn to use teaching tools which they can evaluate with the help of professional personnel and, later, by themselves. It would also be helpful to bring together outside and in-house teachers several times during the year to exchange information, suggestions, and techniques.

In fact, during the first semester of the Community Free School's operation, outside instructors were invited to attend a series of meetings with the teachers of the first house. The teachers from the business community discovered in sharing their concerns with their fellow teachers that their own problems were not unique. They found that even the professional teachers faced some of the same problems. A survey of outside instructors showed that a majority would be willing to attend an in-service training program for one to three hours a week. Such a program has recently been developed but has yet to be tested in practice.

Typical Days

The following "typical days" section recounts the daily experiences of two students and a teacher in the Community Free School. Each is an anecdotal record of a fairly representative day of these two participants. While there are, of course, many other students and teachers who had different daily experiences, the two included here are representative of the majority, at least in terms of the form of their activities, if not the content. The rosters included illustrate the possible courses and activities available in the Community Free School. Re-rostering was done several times during the year, so that each student's and teacher's roster was likely to change at least once or twice during this period.

From a Community Free School Teacher's Notebook

8:00 A.M.: On the way to school . . .

I met one of my former students at West Philadelphia High School going on the bus today and she said, "Oh, kids tell me the Community Free School is great. They say that there are unlimited cuts and teachers don't care if you come to class or not." Now she was saying this with enthusiasm; but she seems to be saying that teachers don't care. If we don't check up on the students if they aren't coming to class, they think we don't care. I think firmness about this would be interpreted by the kids as a sign of caring about them, about the fact that they come to school.

8:30 A.M.: Arrive at school, join another teacher supervising swimming at university gymnasium.

When I was swimming, kids came up to me to ask about things, how to do certain kinds of strokes. One boy whom I'd had in a class at

101

West Philadelphia High, who had been very difficult, hostile, distant and hard for me to talk to, came over and started asking me about 'kicking'. He was really open and eager to learn, even though he was a little defensive when I gave him suggestions. He tried them out and laughed and said he wasn't going to try it again, but I know he will. The thing that's of real importance to me is that he swam all the way across the pool to approach me and ask me some questions about swimming. . .

9:30 A.M.: Return to school, work in reading and writing workshop with two teachers, 35 students.

The reading and writing workshop is a welcome change for the kids. They love the programmed materials. Many who are not rostered in a particular workshop come in anyway. We started with comprehensive tests this week to find out where the students are. They're doing an overwhelming amount of writing; all students have written several things which we are storing in their folders. We're trying to get the students to read longer works, write longer things. They are willing now to write more. We use worksheets to work out the student's particular writing errors.

11:00 A.M.: Free hour — individual conference.

In most of my individual conferences, I have to work with four or five students in an hour. Now this may seem quite ample time to work with four or five students, but this week it's happened to me on numerous occasions that you get into something with a student. Today, for example, one girl got into extremism — political extremism; she wanted to know what the right and left meant; what radical and conservative meant, and how that fit in with other people she had been reading about in the papers. She was into something and we were discussing it and she was interested. . .but I didn't have enough time to work with her because I had four other kids waiting for me — I see possibilities for using many more college students in the Community Free School in very productive kinds of ways — specifically individual conferences.

11:30 Free Hour: Student Steering Committee meeting.

The Steering Committee got together to discuss the social studies curriculum. We are studying many groups that want radical changes in our society. We will be debating on Friday, whether or not blacks should work all together or mixed with other groups. The students have been interested by the speakers who have come in. . . The Steering Committee members decided that they would like to meet together and make some suggestions about the curriculum. We presented the plan and they made suggestions. I was very pleased with what happened. They met for about 45 minutes saying they liked the ideas the teachers had for the week, but also wanted to add their own, and made a list of six points they would like added, including the addition of a policeman to the speaking schedule; since they already heard from the Black Panthers, why not hear a policeman, too?

12:00 Lunch: Family Group meeting with 14 students.

Today we decorated the room. I really sensed the different relationship between me and the kids at the Community Free School. Many of the students are troublemakers; I know this by what they've said and the reputations that they have. Some didn't even go to school before. The fact that they're here and working on something in a group is really exciting.

Today in Family Group I proposed a camping trip. They were more excited about it than I have seen them about anything. They were really excited and wanted to go camping. We are going to try and plan this for next weekend, and we will be anxious to see how it goes, but I have seldom seen such excitement and I'm anxious to plan the camping trip with the students and see how successful it can be.

1:00 P.M.: Social studies class, with one other teacher and 20 students.

The students are now putting together a booklet citing all the community organizations they have visited in this special social studies course. They are taking pictures and each student is writing up a description of one organization. Hopefully they'll get this published through the university, and this will be a resource book for other students in the course and the school, telling them where they can go either to give time or to get services from community organizations. Very importantly, too, I feel this gives the students in the course a sense of what they've accomplished. The tangible evidence of a booklet is something the students can take pride in — and seeing their names in print is very important.

One of the assets of the Free School all along has been the team-teaching technique, a situation which has given us a chance to learn from one another. I think it's been an invaluable experience myself. That we have been able to work together so well especially in planning curriculum is coming out now. We feel comfortable with each other, which I think is important for the students to know, that the teachers get along and can teach together in the classes without ego conflicts. We do work together as a team. . .

3:00 P.M.: Teachers' meeting.

All the teachers have been working 15 hours a day, including Saturday, and today, to get things together for the Community Free School. We have been rostering yesterday and today with computer sheets; we find out, after having spent a whole weekend, that the computer program was not relevant to our situation; we could have done it more easily by hand. I resent this kind of mismanagement. We don't mind putting in extra amounts of work if in fact this work is necessary and worthwhile.

4:30 P.M.: On the way out the door.

I found R. in the hall after school today looking really sad; she'd been looking sad all day. I asked her if something was wrong, and big tears started to roll down her cheeks. So I asked her what was wrong, and she didn't know. It was just this general unhappiness and malaise that finally turned out to be all the really universal problems that adolescents have with particular difficulties that I think are probably common to kids in the Community Free School. I had the feeling that she really wanted to get something off her chest and wanted someone to unload her feelings to. So I tried alternately waiting, letting her come to whatever she had to say about herself without pushing and pulling too much and then, when I felt it was appropriate, I tried just mentioning experiences I'd had that were similar some time or other. . .

One thing she said was that she had no privacy at home; her sister worked and all of her sister's kids, her nephews and nieces, were her responsibility at home, even though they were supposed to be her mother's. But the job fell to her. Later on, I suggested that maybe part of the unhappiness and uncertainty she was feeling had to do with the strangeness and newness of everything at the Community Free School. That really seemed to provoke a response of recognition from her.

I wouldn't be surprised if this newness weighed on kids more than we thought — being at these strange places that are far from what they're accustomed to, having to find hidden buildings in the community, and going on their own. All of that takes independence and a kind of inner personal strength that I'm not sure many of these kids have had a chance to develop. I think we have to really be careful not to overestimate their maturity.

I really believe, though, that this is one of the advantages of the Community Free School: to spend the kind of additional emotional strain of the kids' pouring out that kind of feeling to you. It's a much more whole and human kind of environment.

From Community Free School Students

Student I

Math: I feel that my math has been improved even though my test score didn't improve that greatly. I have a better understanding of the different ways of doing math. I like working alone and at my own speed. . . my teachers are learning to become better teachers as far as I'm concerned.

Reading and Writing Workshop: L.J.S. and S. are very good teachers; you have a better chance of learning because they don't tell you how to learn, they give you the work and explain it the best way possible, then you are to do it the best way you can — and this is the best way to learn.

Family Group: My spirits brightened when we were allowed to write and paint on the wall. I enjoyed this and I think other people did too.

The evaluations are mostly fair. . . there's no sense trying to get credit for something you didn't do. I'd rather have evaluations than grades. . .report cards are like an honor roll. . .leads to competition. . .if it hadn't been for the free school I would have dropped out. I couldn't stand the "A," "B" pressure. If we had grades here I'd be right on top. I'd be average at WPHS. I work harder here because I'm doing the stuff I want to do.

Free Time: People here began to change. They began to show themselves things you wouldn't know about them are in the open. . . everyone knows everyone. You know everybody's business even if you mind your own. It's more like a family — I like it.

Social Studies: I have a course called social science. It's not like a regular social studies class. You go out into community fields. For instance, every Thursday from 1 to 3:30 we visit different city organizations. We've been down to the courthouse, sat in on court hearings, we've been to the public assistance agencies, the health center, where we talked to the staff about their new city program where citizens with medical and psychological problems come for free help. We went to city hall, went to the Afro Aims shop, and talked about how business is set up in a black community, like a black store, how they got the necessary funds to put on this kind of project. Then, on Thursday night we write up papers, and on Friday we come back to the Community Free School, sit down and discuss what we got out of the day before, if we felt it was relevant, if not why, how could it be improved, and where to go next. Another day of the week we work for a city organization. I worked for eight weeks at the Urban League of Philadelphia. It was just like a job, I came and left at a certain time, I worked for them, attended meetings, did papers, set up their newsletter; but, I didn't get paid. My pay was being in an organization, seeing how it works, then getting an evaluation. This is the different type of learning atmosphere that you have here that you don't have at West Philadelphia High School.

Steering Committee: I expected the Community Free School to be like West. But to my amazement I found the main body operating this school was the students. They had group representatives going to meetings, coming up with ideas and suggestions . . . the student makes his own decisions and changes his own classes, but he has to go to them and not cut because he picked his interests and what he wanted when he chose his classes.

. . .the students are allowed to have a say in the affairs of the school, and I think it's great that we have a say in school matters.

Student 2

Outside Course: If you decided you wanted to be something, you had a chance to go into the field, to look and see if this was what you wanted or not. Now I'm enrolled in a computer course at the University City Science Center. The six of us meet with three sets of two teachers each. . .then on other days we have individual meetings. We learn computer programming, basic skills, computer math, computer science. Before you learn the language you have to learn to keypunch, use the Datel, have knowledge of operations, the card-reader, the card-sorter, and different machines which coincide with computer work.

Lunch: It's just so noisy up here. It's quiet now, but that's because nobody's here. When I feel like learning something, there's just too much going on, too much noise. It's not that the House is too crowded — it's that those who are here make too much noise. I don't know what to do about it.

Conference: At West Philadelphia High School there were just too many people. Now I can sit down and talk about special things. Some people I talk with about books, others about what I did over the weekend. I talk to the teachers all the time — about what I want to do, what I think we should do in class, what I dislike about what we do in class. We have a period when you come in and just rap to the teachers. Up at West you never had conferences like that.

Reading and Writing Workshop: For me reading and writing is the first time I have enjoyed English. We read books and write papers on them. My vocabulary has been strengthened, my reading and writing ability has been strengthened.

Math: I have learned more than I could take, but I took it.

Teachers' Meeting: We tell the teachers what we don't like. In reading and writing workshop, we told the teachers we didn't think we were learning. They got the whole House together and asked what students didn't like. They said that we didn't see concrete things we had learned. So the teachers thought about a new program. It started about 3 weeks ago. I like it better now. It can't happen fast, though . . .

Free Time: A Case Study

The PASS Model included in its provisions for an innovative educational program free time periods during the week when the student is permitted freedom of movement and activity. The inclusion of free time in each student's roster is based on the premise that students, like all human beings, need personal time during the day when they are responsible for their own activities; by giving the student this opportunity and responsibility, he will learn to become responsible for himself and his actions.

The inclusion of free time represented one of the most significant departures from traditional educational models and concepts. During the first months of implementation, all groups involved in the Community Free School supported the concept of free time; teachers, administrators, and members of the community board all worked together in attempting to bring this part of the program successfully into being. However, as the problems relating to this aspect of the program multiplied, different groups qualified and modified their support, ultimately changing their attitudes toward free time altogether. The following account of the events involved in the implementation of the free time concept represents a detailed case study of the kind of organizational and administrative crisis which can develop in a community free school, and the results of a departure from the conscientious practice of process leadership. (See p. 123 for an explanation of this concept.)

March, 1970: Problems first arose two months after the Community Free School opened, when it became apparent that few if any students were using their free time for productive purposes. Students spent free time periods playing cards, making noise, disrupting classes, bothering local merchants in the neighborhood, and simply loitering inside or outside the school building. Students also tended to extend their free time periods to the surrounding class periods, either arriving late at their next classes or not attending their classes at all. Community board members took the initiative in responding to this problem; they spoke to students who were cutting class and to their parents and attempted to impress upon them the importance of the students' responsibility in making the school work. Teachers also encouraged students to assume responsibility for this problem; in response, a student judicial board was established for the purpose of dealing with class cutting from within the student body.

April, 1970: Despite these efforts to deal with cutting, free time remained a problem. Some board members, sensitive to community reactions to an apparent discipline problem, were in favor of eliminating free time periods for students and tightening up school discipline. When the problem was put before the community board in April, three alternatives were presented: 1) eliminate free time, 2) allow the existing situation to continue, or 3) restructure free time. The directors of the school and the chairman of the community board persuaded the members to select the third choice. In doing so, the chairman once again emphatically stated her support of the concept: "I think in some of these cases we're definitely getting away from the traditional hangups of the school system. . . This free time should be permitted."

In response to the community board's decision, a recreation room with facilities for a variety of activities was set up, staffed by school personnel. This program operated successfully for two days, and the concept of free time seemed vindicated. Unfortunately, Community Free School personnel found it an increasing burden to perform their regular duties and also staff the recreation room.

May, 1970: Teachers then asked the community board for more help with the program, either in recruiting community volunteers, e.g., parents, or by participating in the recreation program themselves. Since previous experience had demonstrated that free time was feasible under certain conditions, the community board now had to decide whether to actively seek support for the recreation program or to allow the existing situation to continue. While they realized that free time periods could work and did agree to seek help from parents and other community members, the community board never actively sought this help. What they did, in essence, was allow the issue to slide. In field notes from this period, teachers noted with concern that the board was not providing leadership in solving this problem.

September, 1970: When school resumed in the fall, the problem of free time remained. Students were still given free time periods but had no activities or guidance in how to use this time. Once again, merchants complained that students were loitering in their stores; some students disrupted classes in their houses and in other units of the school. Although board members were increasingly concerned and alarmed, no concrete action was taken by them.

More importantly, the community board was reluctant to deal with the problem as members felt it was not within the realm of their responsibilities. The school having been established, some members of the board saw questions of curriculum and discipline as areas of the staff's responsibility. Yet, at the same time, the board did not provide the staff with the authority and wherewithal to solve such problems. In this case, when parents and community volunteers might have provided guidance for students' free time activities, the members of the board who were community residents did not seek these volunteers or encourage parent participation.

October, 1970: At this point, parent dissatisfaction and complaints of neighboring merchants forced the board to make a decision. What they did was to eliminate free time entirely, stating that it had not worked and was not feasible.

The controversy over free time, when viewed in the perspective of the overall Community Free School program, was not a critical indicator of the success or failure of the school. While these problems developed, other aspects of the program proceeded to be successfully implemented, and the school itself continued to operate on a day-to-day basis. However, the issue of free time did lead to a crisis which should be carefully analyzed in hopes that in the future this kind of confrontation can be avoided in the implementation process of community free schools. Also note that the implementation of free time or of the free choice of attending classes is also causing severe problems in most of the schools which have attempted to institute such alternatives into the educational program. *

The initial failure of the free time concept suggests that the PASS Model itself needs to be modified. While it was expected that students would have trouble integrating free time into their educational experience, the extent and magnitude of the problem was not anticipated. The concept of a free school and a flexible curriculum was new enough to students who were used to traditional rules, regulations, and requirements. The inclusion of unstructured periods in student rosters went several steps further than that, asking not only that students select options, but also that they design their own options.

---

*Paul Lauter, "The Short and Happy Life of the Adams-Morgan Community School Project, Harvard Educational Review 38:2 (Spring, 1968), 235-262.

This was clearly too much for students to absorb all at once, and their exuberant response soon transcended the limits of acceptable behavior.

Yet the problem of free time could have been resolved through sustained consultation between teachers, the staff leaders, and members of the community board. Recommendations made during the year included temporary restrictions on free time, a reduction of the number of free periods, acquiring facilities and organizing a recreational program, and enlisting community supervisors or hiring additional staff, more effective student involvement. It is more than likely that one or more of these recommendations, if adopted and conscientiously implemented, might have solved the problem to the satisfaction of all involved. However, the option that was ultimately adopted — elimination of free time — did not reflect the attitudes and expectations of many participants in the school community. Instead, members of the community board effectively took matters into their own hands and looked for help to the traditional school systems and a traditional solution. While the school continued to operate much as it had before, the decision by the community board to eliminate free time set a precedent for autocratic decision-making and problem solving which continued to reverberate for the remainder of the year.

CHAPTER IV

RESEARCH AND EVALUATION

RESEARCH AND EVALUATION

The importance of ongoing research and evaluation cannot be overstressed. In the kind of dynamic learning process which we understand the alternative school to be, ongoing evaluation is essential to the development of an educational program which is responsive to the needs of the students and should therefore be an integral part of the learning program. Continuous feedback to students, teachers, and others involved in the school is also essential if an alternative school is to create and sustain the kind of commitment it requires from all who participate in it.

There is another important reason for building research and evaluation processes into the model of an alternative school. Such schools are frequently called upon to justify their existence in terms of the improved learning experiences of their students. Many such schools which have not built evaluative processes into their design fall victim to budget cuts and other problems of the public system as a result of their inability to state explicitly what they have done for students that traditional schools have not been able to do.

While it is quite common to find self-reflection and criticism in an alternative school of the informal/open type, there is often at the same time a strong resistance to systematic research and evaluation. Part of this resistance may be attributed to the fact that such schools are often asked or required to use traditional means of educational evaluation such as standardized testing. Indeed, educators have traditionally relied almost exclusively on experimental methods and models drawn from psychology.

We believe that multiple research and evaluation techniques should be used in the study of the effectiveness of alternative schools. Statistical data from tests and questionnaires is, of course, still useful in certain specific areas of the educational program. More important for the evaluation of alternative educational programs, however, are the naturalistic techniques of observation and/or participant observation, methods which anthropologists and ethnologists have used successfully for decades. Indeed, these methods are particularly applicable to such schools in that students are not assumed to proceed in learning at a rate which correlates with their chronological age or their position in the educational system. Moreover, alternative educational programs assume that all students have a natural aptitude for learning that does not necessarily fit into traditional teaching methods, whose worth is most often measured by standardized testing techniques. The alternative school assumes that students learn in a variety of ways which may not always be visible to the instructor or even to the student himself. Given a choice, however, the student may gravitate to the learning-teaching methods best suited to his abilities and inclinations. Thus, a great deal takes place in the alternative school in terms of learning and in terms of interaction which cannot always be tapped by traditional techniques. Observational techniques coupled with quantitative data offer some promise of providing us with information not only about the ways in which students learn but also the circumstances and situations which are most conducive to learning and to fruitful interaction.

A model for a school includes a series of related goals and objectives which that school seeks to accomplish. While some of these goals are intangible, others can be measured and evaluated. During the early phases of the Community Free School's existence, data was systematically collected under three categories:

1. Anecdotal/analytical data including teachers' field notes, staff field notes, interviews with individual teachers and with groups of teachers, interviews with students.

2.   Testing: longitudinal data collected by reading tests, College Board Examinations, College Board Writing Sample, Iowa test, and others.

3.   Archival data: attendance in school and in classes; minutes, tape recordings and summaries of teacher and staff meetings; minutes of community board meetings; memoranda, and correspondence.

One difficult problem we found in the West Philadelphia Community Free School was the resistance of the community board to these types of evaluation. The members of the board, among others, feared that their children would be used as guinea pigs for an experiment that might or might not succeed. Another problem was the reluctance of teachers to keep systematic field notes and to see the importance of ongoing evaluation. The most serious problem, however, was the attitude of school system personnel who sat on the community board as well as of the board itself that nothing negative could be said about the school. Therefore, they did not permit any real effort at data gathering. When data was in fact gathered and analyzed and presented in the form of a progress report, board members saw these reports, when they were partially negative, as an attack on the school and refused to allow them to be used as a basis for improvement and change.

During the first phases of any alternative program, ongoing process evaluation must take place on a systematic basis. Such evaluation will bring out the strong points of the program as well as the weak points. Some of this evaluative material will deal with specific aspects of the program and with specific goals. An example from the Community Free School is the specific evaluation which was set up to rearrange the entire inside program of the school. The data sources used for this evaluation were teachers' discussions and notes, students' discussions and notes, video tapes and photographs of activities and classes taking place within the house. The main areas of evaluation were the following: 1) student response, attitude and behavioral change, development of skills, 2) teacher perception of attitudinal and behavioral change, and 3) the effect of the new afternoon program on the morning program. As the results of this evaluative study were analyzed, the information was fed back to the school community to begin making changes. Other areas of analysis can be much more theoretical and should perhaps be conducted by someone who is only partially affiliated with the school. The following two sections deal with this kind of theoretical evaluation and analysis. Although the material for these sections was gathered during the operation of the first three phases of the West Philadelphia Community Free School, they were written after the authors were no longer directors of the school.

TEACHER ADAPTABILITY

Teachers in the new Community Free School were faced with an enormous challenge in implementing the educational program. They had to help 200 randomly selected students adapt from a traditional, structured learning environment to an informal one permitting and encouraging self-exploration. The responsibility of developing a curriculum which would interest students, encourage them to work in the new environment, and respond to their varying academic needs was also the responsibility of the teachers. These demands called for considerable adaptation on the part of the teachers. An analysis of how they responded is reported in the following section, a large part of which is taken from "Teacher Adaptation to an Informal School."*

According to the PASS Model, the teacher's role is "to view learning from the learner's perspective." Of the ten teaching criteria listed, (see p.28) nine are specifically related to the teacher's ability to help students assume responsibility for their own learning. It was therefore significant that in their applications all 15 teachers selected to work full-time in the Community Free School expressed a primary concern for the student in the new environment. More specifically, they expressed a desire to overcome the negative effects of traditional education on students, improve student-teacher relationships, and make education relevant to the student.

The first month of school brought teachers and students into close and sustained contact. For both groups, the break with tradition was sharp and difficult. Students, as might be expected, reacted with bewilderment to the demands of the unfamiliar environment and activities. Teachers, too, found the experience disconcerting and were concerned about the students' confused response to the program.

---

*Aase Eriksen, "Teacher Adaptation to an Informal School," NAASP *Bulletin*, Summer 1972.

Teachers without previous experience in the school system were appalled by students' severe deficiencies in basic skills; other teachers were dismayed by students' inability to analyze material to distinguish between goals and means, and to make choices between simple alternatives.

The response of many teachers was to blame themselves for this initial confusion, attributing student failures to their own personal failures as teachers. Consequently, some teachers found themselves responding in traditional ways, providing structures and direction they had hoped students would develop on their own. But this response was contrary to the objectives the teachers had expressed when choosing to work in the Community Free School, and teachers chastised themselves for this tendency to impose structure.

Seeking relief from their confusion, teachers naturally turned to each other as the most logical and accessible sources of help. Therefore, the most immediate function of teacher interaction at the school was to provide assurance and support to those who needed it. Such interaction provided a positive means of locating the source of a problem, defining its nature and extent, and searching for possible solutions. During the first month, teacher interaction was critically important because it allowed teachers to share their initial experiences and deal with their frustrations as a group. Subsequently, interaction became the primary process for decision-making and the basic operating principle of the school.

Over 75% of combined teaching hours in the first term were spent in teams ranging in size from two to four teachers and consisting of both regular teachers and graduate interns. The teacher-student ratio was small. Although there was variation in both team and class size, a typical team-taught class would consist of one regular teacher, two graduate interns, and 35 students. Often the class would separate into small groups, with one teacher responsible for each group. Small-group work in teams represents the first step away from the traditional classroom.

Teachers noted that in a classroom so organized it was possible to plan and evaluate the class as a team and to work effectively with individuals in the small groups. The size of the team-taught class allowed teachers to work in both large and small groups and to experiment with various approaches to the same subject, geared to the different needs and academic levels of the students.

Team-taught classrooms were not without problems. When several teachers led a class together, they sometimes found themselves contradicting each other and consequently confusing the students. The problem of delegating responsibility among teachers for team-taught classes, developed four to six-week minicourses, and worked in cross-disciplinary teams.

During the second year of the program the number of houses, students, certified teachers, and graduate interns all expanded. Teachers worked in a variety of team-teaching situations; they planned shorter classes, developed four to six-week minicourses, and worked in cross-disciplinary teams.

One house developed an integrated curriculum consisting of a series of team-taught and individually taught classes which combined disciplines. Teachers in this house felt they had developed a process for interaction which enabled them to work simultaneously in groups and by themselves, within and between disciplines. They felt confident in all of these situations and continued to plan and evaluate the overall program together.

An innovation of the team approach, planned and adopted by teachers in all three houses, was the reading and writing workshop which was designed to be part of the humanities program. Teachers planned and evaluated the workshops constantly during the year. Through a process of adaptation and change, they developed methods of interaction which enabled them to give attention to individual students, keep track of where students were heading, and continue working together in planning and teaching.

A certain amount of "natural selection" took place among the teachers due to the flexibility of the educational program. While the majority of teachers taught in teams, several continued to teach alone during the first term. Teachers who had trouble working as part of a large team divided into smaller teams. Teaching schedules varied, and teachers spent at least one fourth of their time outside the classroom in conference with individual students. Family groups met at the discretion of the teachers and students involved. The flexibility of the program and the varied teaching schedules also permitted teachers to visit other classrooms and participate in other team situations.

Planning and evaluation meetings were held frequently. House teachers meetings were held weekly, and teachers met in small groups during the day, in the evening, and on weekends when necessary. Students were invited to sit in on afternoon sessions among teachers to exchange ideas and criticisms. In the beginning and on occasion throughout the year, some teachers felt a hesitancy to express themselves freely in front of students, especially in regard to teaching and the educational program. They feared such discussion might convey an unfair and pessimistic impression of the school, its teachers, and students.

All teachers recognized the potential of the open meetings, despite the misgivings of some. Free and open discussion could be a means for improving student-teacher relationships, clearing up misunderstandings, and encouraging the same kind of interaction to develop among students. Teachers recognized that attempts by them to interact could be a learning experience for both participating teachers and students. Therefore, the open meetings continued with students observing, asking questions, and offering suggestions.

The principal criticism resulting from their self-examination was that teachers were not spending enough time planning together. The year had begun without a clearly defined plan for the curriculum. This was partly a result of initial expectations that students would participate in planning the program. However, teachers were obliged to assume most of the responsibility for planning during the first semester. Consequently, they needed to spend a great deal of time with each other as well as with the students. This time was not always available, and, as a result, it was sometimes hard for teachers to stay ahead of their classes.

Evaluating their progress at the end of the first semester, some teachers felt they had been able to work well together, especially in curriculum planning and in helping their students progress. Other, more critical teachers felt an urgent need to communicate more effectively, to devise processes for planning more effectively, and to have more time to work together.

The importance of the teaching unit was established beyond question at the end of the first term. Seven out of eight certified teachers and all of the graduate interns (as full time teachers) applied to remain in the school. As stated by one teacher, the Community Free School, unlike traditional high schools, had provided an environment in which three new kinds of teacher interaction took place: in planning curriculum, in evaluating the strengths and weaknesses of the program, and in coordinating and implementing daily activities. Despite problems encountered within each of these processes, teachers felt that progress had been made and were unanimous in requesting that the original faculty group be retained in order to build on the experiences of the first semester.

Students were also anxious that the teaching staff remain intact. Their concern was based not only on loyalty to particular teachers, but also on the feeling of belonging to a fairly cohesive and integrated family unit in which teachers, despite internal quarrels, understood and supported them.

The teachers' growing concern with the teaching staff as a whole reflects an important shift in their priorities. From an initial focus on the student-teacher relationship, teachers began to place more and more emphasis on relationships among each other. They realized that the task of helping students adjust to the school environment and meeting their wide range of educational needs was too great for teachers to accomplish as individuals.

Analysis of data pertaining to teachers' experiences at the West Philadelphia Community Free School reveals that teachers as well as students needed time to adapt to the informal environment. Teachers never reached a point where they were satisfied with the effectiveness of their interaction, nor did they ever assert that the school's objectives had been achieved. However, by the end of the first three semesters, they were enthusiastic about the potential of the program and anxious to continue developing and improving their work as a group. The process of developing effective methods of teacher interaction proved to be a difficult one; however, teachers recognized that their own need to adapt to the informal environment was a prerequisite to the school's success and that increasing the extent and variety of interaction among teachers provided the means for that adaptation.

PROCESS LEADERSHIP*

In the implementation of a new educational program, strains and pressures inevitably occur. To withstand these tensions and initial shocks, school staff members must be able to rely upon one another. They must develop personal and professional means of interaction which enable them to work effectively as a group. Strong leadership is required to initiate and sustain educational innovation; yet equally important, in the long run, is the delegation of authority to staff members, and the assumption of responsibility for the program by all involved in its implementation.

Traditional models for leadership and responsibility in public schools are largely inadequate when applied to alternative schools and, in particular, an alternative school that is seen as a community in itself. Thus, this section describes what has been called process leadership: a dynamic situation in which all participants share leadership responsibilities, and, at the same time, look to certain designated leaders for guidance in circumstances that require it. It is essential that assumptions underlying process leadership motivate the behavior of all responsible members of the school community: the community board, the directors, the community coordinator, teachers, and students as they perform leadership functions at various times and as they carry on their duties in the daily operation of the school.

An alternative school is a continuing experiment whose participants create their own alternatives for action based on the concrete and theoretical goals which they have set out to achieve. Action takes the form best suited to deal with the particular circumstances, individuals, and groups. The director, therefore, operates under one given only, and that is to implement the educational model which the community desires for its children. His established and unchanging task is to perpetuate an educational philosophy in an operating school. And the continuing operation of the school is what is of primary and ultimate importance, for only in this context can the necessary experimentation take place. The theoretical model sets up the general framework but

---

*This section is adapted from an article, "The Dynamics of Leadership in an Informal School," by Aase Eriksen and Judith Messina, *Journal of Research and Development in Education* (Spring, 1972).

does not specify the procedures necessary for its achievement. These, therefore, must be developed by all participants as the school actually functions.

Although the leader maintains a hierarchical position, he does not derive his legitimacy from that position or from the greater system of which he is part as in the case of the traditional public school administrator. Rather, the director of an alternative school derives his authority from his ability to influence others. He has no sanctions or rewards to bestow upon teachers and students, for, according to the community free school model, mistakes are indicators of the need for change not signs of negligence or of the failure to comply with already established regulations and procedures. The director's legitimacy derives from the demonstration of his expertise as well as from his behavior toward other participants. He is himself a model as well as a participant, and, for this reason, there are no limits to the scope of his activities. Indeed, it is essential that the director demonstrate his willingness and ability to perform those things he asks of others. So much so that eventually students and teachers of the Community Free School saw it as natural and even expected that the director should help them clean and paint their houses as well as teach a course.

Crucial to the spirit of experimentation is the teachers' ability to perceive mistakes and change not as failure or as the result of failure but as necessary steps toward the accomplishment of the goals — a process of development in themselves, in the students, and in the school. Teachers at first relied greatly upon the director as he had the leader's title as well as the expertise to guide them in an unfamiliar situation. None of them could have anticipated the daily problems that would crop up as the school program got underway, but they expected as much of themselves as they felt the director expected of them. So, in the beginning, they saw these daily problems as their own failures, failing not only themselves, but the director, the students, and the community. Gradually though, teachers did acquire more self-confidence and the ability to effect and cope with change without a sense of guilt or failure.

In an alternative school, teachers are responsible not only for their students and the activities of their classrooms, but they also take a major part in the decisions which affect the ongoing operation of the entire school. In the beginning of the second semester of the Community Free School program, a computer was used to do the individual rostering of students. As teachers began to work with the computer schedule, however, they found it unrealistic and unfeasible. Consequently, they took upon themselves the task of restructuring the entire roster and worked with other staff members for many hours over one weekend in order to make each roster suit the needs and interests of individual students.

There will be times in the implementation when teachers are unable or unwilling, sometimes due to the sheer amount of energy required, to make certain decisions or to accept responsibility for even greater change. For instance, the director continually urged teachers and students to paint and decorate their houses. The students of one unit even painted their house twice. The initial work begun in the other two houses, however, soon stopped and was left unfinished as were several other projects in each of the houses. Finally, during the summer, students and teachers in one of the houses spent several weeks repainting and decorating when they had more time and energy to devote to this project.

For the sake of morale and in order for the school to continue to operate, someone must be able to make decisions on short notice and to take personal responsibility for them. This is the director's task. Although he can and will make decisions without the benefit of group opinion or discussion, his decisions are always subject to revision when the group as a whole is willing and able to deal with them. In the Community Free School, there were continual informal and spontaneous meetings among teachers, students, and the director and his assistants. The offices were always open and all knew they were welcome to come in and talk or work there. Teachers did not hesitate to call the director at home if there was some matter to discuss or a problem to solve.

In a school which seeks alternative ways of doing all sorts of things, there is also needed someone who can and is willing to take the risks necessary to keep the school in operation. This means cutting through red tape, going around individuals in their official capacities, and perhaps antagonizing others to provide what is best for the continued operation of the school and for the well-being of the participants. The director of the Community Free School, for instance, risked antagonizing officials at the board of education in order to have graduate interns (who had taught one semester at the school and who worked well there) rehired as regular teachers for the following year. It is unrealistic to ask teachers to take similar risks, especially in the beginning of the implementation when they are themselves only learning how to act in alternative ways. By taking such risks the leader, moreover, demonstrates his commitment to the educational philosophy and to the participants in the alternative school. He engenders their trust and respect, and, again, acts as a model for them in their own learning process.

The leader also ensures that the theoretical guidelines of the model are adhered to. It is his job to evaluate the implementation process and to recognize deviations from the goals of the model. Here, he must make a judgment as to whether a deviation is simply one of method or whether it implicitly contradicts the goals of the educational philosophy.

Because his role is one of dealing with individuals on a personal and informal level, the director is subject to great stress and inevitably bears the larger share of responsibility for the operation of the school. In stressful situations, the public school administrator tends to feel he must know everything that happens in the school because he is accountable to his superiors for whatever may occur there. It is this feeling of the need to know everything that can make for feelings of guilt and secrecy on the part of teachers and other staff members particularly if mistakes are seen as failures. By contrast, the process leader does not and should not feel he must know everything. His own actions are based on trust in the competence of others to make decisions and to perform their jobs well. Knowing everything only complicates his job and adds to the number of tasks, particularly administrative tasks, that he must perform.

At the same time, however, the director also needs support in a personal sense as well as in his leadership role. Experience in the Community Free School has shown that one form this support may take is in the form of two assistants who also have decision-making power in certain areas, thereby creating a leadership team. These assistants, who were not appointed as teachers but had teaching experience, gained the respect and trust of the teaching staff partly because the director openly relied on them and encouraged the teachers to do so also. These assistants also acted as a safety valve for the director and teachers and students. They filtered information, when they felt it necessary or important, to the director. In some cases, teachers merely verbalized their frustrations to them in order to relieve anxiety and tension. At other times, it was understood that the information would reach the director, particularly in cases where teachers had perceived their own actions as failure. Rather than admitting this perceived failure to the director or confronting the director with complaints, teachers talked to a team member and thus avoided what they felt could have been a stressful situation. Having received such information, the director could then go to the teacher with advice and suggestions softening the blow of what teachers initially felt would be a confrontation.

It is important to note here that the leadership team allows the director himself to function in his role. Relationships between the director and the teachers in the Community Free School would have been more strained and taken longer to develop in an informal way had not the team acted as a safety valve.

The patterns of interaction among the members of the leadership team were as fluid as other patterns and processes in the school. As teachers became more familiar with the director, they discarded their previous notions as to what one tells or does not tell the director and as to the tasks he should perform. Eventually a definite pattern emerged: in cases of crises due to external pressures, teachers went to the director himself; in internal crises, they intended to look either to themselves or to the other members of the leadership team.

As stated above, it is essential that this kind of process leadership be repeated and seen in the behavior of all members of the school community. The individual houses, for instance, work as small schools in themselves, each developing a unique and distinct character based on needs and wishes of the students and teachers in that house.

During the first semester, the stress on the head teacher was great: he was responsible for coordinating the inside educational program and for assisting teachers with their administrative duties; at the same time, he carried a full teaching schedule and consulted regularly with the director and the other members of the school staff. In the fall, when the school expanded to three houses and 500 students, it was clear that a change had to be made; the director could no longer consult as frequently with three head teachers as with one. And although the school staff was enlarged, it was understood that even more responsibility for day-to-day operations would now have to be delegated to house teachers. After consulting with the first head teacher, who expressed his concern that this role was already over burdened, it was decided to assign co-head teachers to each house and to lighten head teachers' class loads. Each pair of head teachers would share the responsibilities for coordination and administration and would meet regularly in a group with the director and staff. During the second year, the roles of the head teachers in relation to each other and to the teaching staff as a whole evolved in different ways and illustrate several weaknesses of the concept of co-equal leadership.

In one house, both leaders were slow to assume the responsibility for making decisions; at the same time, they were not willing to share their problems with their colleagues so that the group might work them out together. Because the environment of the house was on the whole flexible and open, a third teacher assumed responsibility when the head teachers would not or could not. However, because he lacked the authority of the head teachers, he could not bring certain functions and operations to their logical conclusions within the school community. Thus the position of the house was weakened in relation to the other houses.

In the second house, both head teachers were experienced teachers; each had clear beliefs about what he wanted to see done, but they did not fully agree either on the theoretical ends of the model, nor on the means to these ends. Eventually, one head teacher withdrew and concentrated on his work with students. He remained effective in situations involving students but was passive in his relationships with other teachers. The other head teacher was thus left with a massive work load. Fortunately, this head teacher was able to share frustrations and problems with most of the teachers in the house so that a certain amount of responsibility was delegated within the group.

In the third house, one of the head teachers immediately assumed the major responsibility for both of them. In addition, he also maintained a dominant role among his colleagues, failing to share decision-making and problem-solving for the house. His attitude may have been motivated by his role as the most experienced teacher in a house with several teachers who had little or no experience in a community school. It soon became clear, however, that he had assumed an unbearable workload and often showed signs of stress and tension. In addition, the teachers in this third house soon began to feel that they were not participating in the decisions which affected them and the operation of the house. They responded by withdrawing into their own classrooms where they felt they could maintain a sense of responsibility and authority.

These experiences have led to the conclusion that co-head leadership is not feasible in a school of this sort. While the basic philosophy remains democratic, there are circumstances which require the exertion of guidance, authority, and expertise. Such qualities are particularly important in the implementation phase when problems, anxieties, and frustrations are at their height. As far as the position of head teacher is concerned, a better system might be to rotate head teachers each year, so that no one person, no one personal style of leadership would become institutionalized. Indeed, the process of leadership in the Community Free School may be seen as an attempt to avoid the institutionalization of structures beyond their usefulness. It is a philosophy of change within change: the willingness to employ new strategies and new ideas and to view mistakes as necessary, even beneficial, to the person and school community as a whole.

EPILOGUE

To use a popular phrase, this is "the way it was" after the first year at the West Philadelphia Community Free School. Making it through that first year was a milestone. There were many who gave the school little chance of surviving and many who would have liked to see it fold as a victim of unrealistic notions, pedagogical heresies, and amateurish solutions to complex and difficult problems. In a sense, the Community Free School was a David facing an army of Goliaths, and this challenge enabled all those directly involved with the school — businessmen, community residents, university officials, students, teachers, and parents — to work relentlessly for its success.

Things have changed since June 1971, as of course they must. To be effective, a school must change constantly in order to be a responsive and viable institution. It is our belief that the variety of groups which make up such a school must cooperate to develop the school in the ways which most effectively meet the needs of its students. While there are no set solutions to problems, no programmed means of meeting students' needs, and no standard patterns of development, there are critical areas that must be dealt with in the implementation of an alternative school:

1. Learning Environments: size, space, variety, location;

2. Learning Process: informality, curriculum, use of community resources, student participation and responsibility;

3. Socialization Patterning: interaction of individuals and groups within the school community, heterogeneity of students and teachers;

4. Community Partnership: The partners and the nature of the partnership, the structures and responsibilities of the community board, shared goals and objectives;

5. Evaluation: measurement of success against shared goals and objectives.

There are some obvious differences between the original Community Free School and the school as it is today. For example, there are now only two houses which accommodate 300 students instead of three houses. Moreover, teacher interns no longer work in the Community Free School. The inside program has been changed to resemble more closely the regular high school program. Yet, equally important are the similarities that remain. The community board still meets regularly for the development and direction of the school. The atmosphere is still informal. Teachers, for instance, are still called by their first names. On a recent visit to the school at four o'clock one afternoon, we walked into a brightly colored room with tables and desks scattered randomly around. We encountered the familiar scene of teachers and students perched atop desks and sitting comfortably on the carpeted floor, engaged in casual but earnest conversation. The original partnership between the community, the board of education, the University of Pennsylvania, and the business community still exists.

It is always instructive to reflect on what could have been done differently so that some of the more troublesome problems and glaring mistakes might have been avoided. The sense of urgency in implementing the program tended to aggravate the problems that were already inherent in setting up an experimental school. More specifically:

1. More time was needed in order to learn from and correct mistakes made initially. There was also needed a feeling of sufficient support from all the partners to allow for the agonizing process of correcting initial mistakes and misconceptions. Participants in the development of an alternative school need to understand that the desire for immediate, demonstrable successes can preclude the admission of failures and the action needed to correct them. For example, to reach a student who has spent ten years in a traditional school, to begin to change his attitudes and behavior, and for him to believe that the goals and methods of the Community Free School are capable of meeting his personal needs and desires take many months.

    There is always great pressure on an experimental school to produce dramatic and virtually instantaneous results, to radically alter behavior and attitudes that have been a long time in the making and that are firmly entrenched. Although it is unlikely that future projects of this sort will be relieved of such pressures, it is essential to state explicitly that expectations of dramatic and instant change are not only unrealistic but are also potentially fatal to such an experiment.

2. Despite the tremendous pressure from all sides to relieve the overcrowding at the mother school, more time for planning should have been built into the project. The Community Free School project was conceived in August and was expected to be in operation by November. Even the extension to a February opening required a great expenditure of time and energy. Participants were expected in three months time (with the extension, six months) to have completed the selection of students and staff, training of staff, orientation of parents and students, the consolidation of relationships among the partners, the selection and development of curriculum, the orientation of the business community and the development of the outside course program, the

selection and renovation of facilities, and the acquisition of equipment, materials and supplies.

3. The school needed to grow gradually. In the beginning the Community Free School opened its doors to 200 students, eight teachers and six graduate interns scattered in several locations, none of them with adequate supplies or materials. In this highly charged and confusing atmosphere daily crises were the rule. Nevertheless, it was during those first months that the decision was made to expand to meet as closely as possible the original time table set by the community board, i.e., to offer space for 1,000 students in five Community Free School houses within one year. Although there was an awareness of the problems inherent in rapid expansion, the urgency to relieve overcrowding at the local school and to meet the expectations of dramatic results persuaded the community board to open two new schools in September, 1971, only six months after the original opening. These two new houses brought the total student body to approximately 500, with 20 teachers and 13 graduate interns.

In retrospect, the optimum strategy would have been to expand more gradually and only after identifying the problem areas and setting up the necessary processes to deal with them.

Despite the changes suggested above, there are many things which would be done in exactly the same way:

1. Significantly, the school would again be opened as quickly as possible without waiting to work out the fine details. While more supplies, better facilities, and greater cooperation would have helped, waiting for everything to be just right would have led to innumerable delays and probably further conflict. Indeed, an excellent strategy for killing enthusiasm and/or an entire project is by not acting at all.

    This may seem contradictory in light of the feeling stated above that there was too little time for planning; yet, it merely points up the important considerations which must be dealt with in the implementation of an alternative school and the trade-offs which must be made in order to meet shared goals and objectives.

2.	The same level of commitment and dedication would be expected from the community board, the teachers, and the students in making the school a viable educational alternative. During the first nine months of the project (September 1969 to June 1970) the community board met every week and sometimes twice a week. It was not at all unusual to see the lights on in one of the houses until eight or nine o'clock at night while groups of teachers worked together developing curriculum, discussing the events of the day, and sharing problems and concerns. On many evenings, students had to be asked to leave the house so that teachers could lock up and go home themselves.

3.	The decision would again be made to give pedagogical goals priority and to fight against compromising them for the sake of political expediency. While politics are inevitable in the implementation and operation of a community school, the school must be given the chance to succeed or fail on its own merits, and pedagogical considerations must remain paramount, as, for example in selecting teachers of the highest caliber. The intervention of politics must be guarded against and neutralized as much as possible.

4.	Finally, participants in the implementation and operation of an alternative school must create the climate for and maintain a willingness to cut through bureaucratic red tape, to break precedent, and to think and act differently.

June 1972 saw the graduation of a group of students who had spent nearly their entire high school careers in the Community Free School. It was these students who had helped define, by their ongoing, daily input, the kind of school the Community Free School was, who watched the school evolve, and who knew better than most what this alternative school was all about.

One student who had cut classes enough at the mother school to be held back a grade the year before wrote that the Community

Free School was one of the six greatest influences on her life, "because it has a lot to offer you if you're interested. Any other school wouldn't lend you a camera or a tape recorder because I don't think they trust you. But the Free School is a place where people trust you."

One teacher noted the enormous change in many of her students:

R., who rarely laughed and only smiled in a painfully shy way, laughs openly now and talks much more freely to other students. While at the beginning she would have been extremely reticent about asking for anything, she now takes the initiative to ask me about the summer computer program or to help her learn how to develop a roll of film to show the boys on the block she was studying. E. was very shy and eager to please, harassed and persecuted by other students in my class at West Philadelphia High School. But at the Free School he really feels that he has a legitimate role in maintaining the school.

For some of the teachers too, June 1972, marked the end of their experiences in the Community Free School. Some of them had decided to go on to graduate school, others were moving to other parts of the country. Some of those who had been there since the school's inception looked back on their experiences and made the following comments:

It really gave me another whole or several more dimensions on the lives of the kids that I would ordinarily just see in a flat perspective in class. It makes me realize all the problems and really kind of overriding feelings that have to be dealt with before classes can really go any place. I really believe that that's one of the advantages of the Free School, to spend the kind of additional emotional strain of kids pouring out their feelings to you. It's a much more whole and human kind of environment.

I feel I must make classes meaningful. This isn't easy and I haven't found any easy answers, but every day I think I learn a little about what is meaningful to the individual, and, hopefully, at the same time achieve some of our objectives as educators and community people.

I feel more human, more able to treat people like individuals, and more able to put my intelligence to some sort of use. I really believe that alternatives like the Free School are essential if people who are teaching because they believe that students can grow through the exchange of ideas and human relationships are to be willing to continue teaching.

APPENDIX A

INSIDE PROGRAM ORGANIZATION

The following points illustrate one way in which the program might be organized in order to meet state requirements and provide for the unique aspects of the program:

1. Family groups rostered from 12 to 1 P.M., Monday, Wednesday and Friday. Tuesday should be left open to give the science program these hours for students who need it. Thursday for all-house meetings, steering committee, etc.

2. Gym: Monday — Wednesday — Friday, 8:30-10 A.M. Each house will use one of these mornings for teacher meetings: Monday — House I, Wednesday — House II, Friday — House III. This leaves two houses in charge of the gym each morning.

3. Hygiene is taught in family groups.

4. Minimum weekly hours as requirement for graduation:

Humanities	7 hours
Science	2 hours
Math (could include business)	4 hours

Foreign language	4 hours
Minimum hours that must be taken in-house:	
Humanities	5 hours
Science	2 hours
Math	2 hours

Foreign language	2½ hours

These minimum requirements can be achieved in various ways, such as class project, group work, conference, and outside courses.

5. Require: 1 outside course
   Encourage: 2 courses

6. School day should be considered to be from 8:30 A.M. to 3:30 P.M.

7.   Total minimum hours for WPCFS.

Humanities — science — math	13 hours
Gym	3 hours
Family groups	5 hours
	21 hours
Including foreign language	4 hours
TOTAL	25 hours

Total minimum hours in-house:

Humanities — science — math	9 hours
Gym and family groups	8 hours
	17 hours
Including foreign language	2½ hours
TOTAL	19½ hours

Minicourse Unit

I.   Ways of Knowing Yourself

II.   Length of Unit: Eighteen hours.

III.   General Information and Comments

This unit is designed as a context for the encouragement and development of basic language skills. We have found that our students are extremely interested in anything that deals with their own personality and the general ways in which people behave. Using this interest as a place to begin, we have developed a course of study that requires the use of specific skills to understand and use information and approaches which the students themselves think important to learn. We must stress that at all times content is subordinate to skills; this is our major concern. It must be realized that this unit has been taught in a highly supportive atmosphere in an inner-city school with extraordinary teacher-pupil relationships. In addition, it was taught to four different classes after January, 1971, and all the people concerned had been interacting for four months. Thus, as an introductory unit with new students, it may be *too* emotionally charged in some activities. We don't know. But it also may be a good way of establishing closer relationships early in the year, if the teachers will go through the activities and open up personally.

In developing and teaching this unit, we have found it important to stress certain central concepts:

1. The use of small groups within the larger class.

2. The importance of the teacher's doing everything he asks the students to do.

3. The use of the small groups as a way to evaluate each other's writing and thinking.

4. The altering of the curriculum as written to meet the needs of students who need special attention or an extra challenge. (Alternatives and extra assignments are presented in comments throughout this unit.)

5. That special attention be paid to the development of abstract operations, such as introspection and analyzing interview data.

Each student will develop individually along these lines. Some will be able to perform abstract operations quite easily; others will need extra help in this area. In some cases, it may be necessary for the teacher to create more concrete manipulative activities for those students who need them. Students should keep all material in a personal folder with a special sheet for new words that come up.

IV. Learning Method Handout

1. Diagnostic	Writing and discussion	
2. Personality Inventory	Small groups, Discussion	No. 1
3. Personality Interview	Small groups, Interviewing, Summarizing & Organizing	No. 2
4. Palmistry	Analyzing a theory by playing a game, "Touch," and writing	No. 3 and No. 4
5. Handwriting Analysis	Introspection by choosing descriptive adjectives, Handwriting analysis from booklet, Writing	No. 5
6. Trust Games	Discussion groups, Sensitivity activities	

7. Body Types	Categorizing, Critical writing	No. 6 and 7
8. Freud	Role playing, Writing	No. 8
9. Jung	Discussion	No. 9
10. ESP	Games	No. 10, 11
11. Astrology	Summarizing	No. 12
12. Dreams	Writing, Interpretation	No. 13, 14 No. 15

V.   Resources and Materials

Materials will be listed with each activity. These will include handouts on the pages which follow each specific activity. In most cases, the handouts can be duplicated by using dittoes and a ditto machine (stencils and a mimeograph machine would serve the same purpose if that is what is available. A xerox machine is expensive for making several copies but would be satisfactory).

For at least one of the activities in the unit, the use of tape recorders is suggested, but alternatives are offered if tape recorders cannot be obtained.

One activity makes use of a commercially distributed game called *Touch* by Parker Brothers ($3.50).

Several books might be used as resource materials if the teacher feels he needs some added background material:

Interpretation of Nature and Psyche. C. S. Jung.
My World of Astrology,   Sidney, Omarr.
Kingdom of Dreams. J. & P. O. Shuyler.

VI. Overall Objectives

A.   Content

1.   To increase student's knowledge of himself;

2.   To present a variety of ways of describing personality;

3. To increase an awareness of one's characteristics, values, ideals and modes of perceiving reality;

4. To understand three systematic notions of personality (Freud, Jung and Sheldon) well enough to apply them to oneself;

5. To understand three popular methods of personality description (palmistry, handwriting analysis, and astrology) well enough to apply them to oneself;

6. To understand two concepts that relate to personality (ESP and dreams) sufficiently to apply them to oneself.

B. Skills

1. To increase proficiency in language and communication skills;

2. To develop the student's ability of introspection and evaluation;

3. To move sequentially from concrete to more abstract thinking;

4. To improve reading skills;

5. To improve writing skills;

6. To improve vocabulary skills and develop a vocabulary suitable for talking about personality;

7. To develop an ability to summarize;

8. To increase abilities to communicate feelings as a result of developing descriptive abilities;

9. To increase usage of metaphoric and symbolic language;

10. To develop interviewing skills;

11. To read and follow directions;

12. To develop manipulative skills in classifying, distinguishing among comparing, and evaluating concrete objects;

13. To develop conceptual reasoning skills in classifying, distinguishing among, comparing, and evaluating abstract ideas;

14. To encourage introspection;

15. To develop listening skills;

16. To hold orderly discussions in which people feel free to speak and to be receptive to others.

OUTSIDE PROGRAM COURSE DESCRIPTIONS

The Law: Everything and All About It

The law can work for you if you know how to use it. Learn the answers to questions like: how does our legal system work, who can you go to to defend your rights, what are the different jobs lawyers and judges perform, does the system work. You'll hear the answers to these questions and come up with answers of your own, too. See trials, talk to judges and young lawyers.

Media and the Urban Environment

Analyzing the role of media within one's personal world, appreciating the importance of media in shaping values, basic nonverbal communication forms, multi-media messages in relation to ideas, feelings, and change. Study of TV, popular music, institutions, community planning, various social organizations, and structures. In-depth probes of specific media, skills, of photography, slide-tape making, motion picture production, some work in portable videotape.

Radiology: X-Ray Diagnosis

Assist staff technologists at Philadelphia General Hospital in x-ray examinations of patients. Perform duties involved in reception of patients and delivery to exam rooms. Functions of Nuclear Medicine Lab, Radiation Physics, Tumor Clinic, X-Ray and Cobalt Therapy, and Stroke Research Neuro-Radiology Lab. Observe radiologists as they interpret radiographs and dictate reports. Assist photographic aides in processing of x-ray film. Instruction in duties involved in x-ray film room. Learn what is involved in the administration and management of a large radiology department, personnel, budgeting, ordering, scheduling.

Bank Operations

Discussion and on-the-job experience in the functions of the banking industry, relation of the bank to the community, job opportunities, employee responsibilities, position of local banks in the industry, training in the areas of division head, operational supervisor, and unit supervisor.

Construction and Maintenance of a Gas Distribution System

Exposure to construction and maintenance activities of a utility having 6,000 miles of underground piping. Emphasis placed on monitoring activities of construction and maintenance workers, equipment and machinery utilization, and inspection of work of outside contractors. Interest in construction, equipment and special machinery, construction work forces, inspectors' responsibility in paving and construction will be rewarded here.

Sample Roster of a Teacher at the West Philadelphia Community Free School
Spring Semester, 1971

	9 - 10	10 - 11	11 - 12	12 - 1	1 - 3
MONDAY	GYM	READING AND WRITING WORKSHOP	READING AND WRITING WORKSHOP (STUDENT PROJECTS)		WAYS OF KNOWING (MINI-UNIT)
TUESDAY	RADICAL POLITICS (MINI-UNIT)	READING AND WRITING WORKSHOP	STUDENT CONFERENCE OR FAMILY GROUP	STUDENT CONFERENCE OR FAMILY GROUP	WAYS OF KNOWING (MINI-UNIT)
WEDNESDAY		READING AND WRITING WORKSHOP	READING AND WRITING WORKSHOP (STUDENT PROJECTS)		WAYS OF KNOWING (MINI-UNIT)
THURSDAY	RADICAL POLITICS (MINI-UNIT)	READING AND WRITING WORKSHOP	STUDENT CONFERENCE OR FAMILY GROUP	STUDENT CONFERENCE OR FAMILY GROUP	LITERATURE
FRIDAY		RADICAL POLITICS (MINI-UNIT)	STUDENT CONFERENCE OR FAMILY GROUP	STUDENT CONFERENCE OR FAMILY GROUP	SPECIAL EVENTS

Sample Roster of a Student at West Philadelphia Community Free School
Spring 1970

Day	9:00–9:30	9:30–10:00	10:00–10:30	10:30–11:00	11:00–11:30	11:30–12:00	12:00–12:30	12:30–1:00	1:00–1:30	1:30–2:00	2:00–2:30	2:30–3:00	3:00–3:30	3:30–4:00
MONDAY	GYM		ALGEBRA			LUNCH		FREE		SECRETARY POOL				
TUESDAY	SOCIAL STUDIES 3				URBAN HEALTH 3		LUNCH		FREE	ENGLISH 5				
WEDNESDAY	GYM		ALGEBRA			ENGLISH 5			LUNCH	TRAV-EL	BANK			
THURSDAY	INSURANCE				TRAV-EL		SOCIAL STUDIES CONFERENCE		LUNCH	SECRETARY POOL				
FRIDAY	GYM		SOCIAL STUDIES 3		URBAN HEALTH		ENGLISH CONFERENCE		LUNCH					

Sample Roster of a Student at West Philadelphia Community Free School
Spring 1970

	9:00 9:30	9:30 10:00	10:00 10:30	10:30 11:00	11:00 11:30	11:30 12:00	12:00 12:30	12:30 1:00	1:00 1:30	1:30 2:00	2:00 2:30	2:30 3:00	3:00 3:30	3:30 4:00
MONDAY	GYM	SPANISH	SPANISH	SPANISH	BIOLOGY	BIOLOGY	BIOLOGY		LUNCH	SOCIAL STUDIES	SOCIAL STUDIES			
TUESDAY	MEDIA AND THE URBAN ENVIRONMENT	MEDIA AND THE URBAN ENVIRONMENT		GEOMETRY	GEOMETRY	GEOMETRY	LUNCH	LUNCH	SOCIAL STUDIES	SOCIAL STUDIES	SOCIAL STUDIES	SOCIAL STUDIES		
WEDNESDAY	GYM	SPANISH	SPANISH	SPANISH	BIOLOGY	BIOLOGY	BIOLOGY		LUNCH	ENGLISH (INDEPENDENT STUDY)	ENGLISH (INDEPENDENT STUDY)			
THURSDAY	ENGLISH 7	ENGLISH 7	ENGLISH 7	GEOMETRY	GEOMETRY	GEOMETRY	LUNCH	LUNCH	MEDIA AND THE URBAN ENVIRONMENT	MEDIA AND THE URBAN ENVIRONMENT	MEDIA AND THE URBAN ENVIRONMENT	MEDIA AND THE URBAN ENVIRONMENT		
FRIDAY	GYM	GYM	ENGLISH 7	ENGLISH 7	LUNCH	LUNCH	SOCIAL STUDIES	SOCIAL STUDIES	INDEPENDENT STUDY	INDEPENDENT STUDY	INDEPENDENT STUDY	INDEPENDENT STUDY		

APPENDIX B

The Administrative Structure of the
West Philadelphia Community Free School

COMMUNITY BOARD

Qualifications: A member of the community board must have made a significant commitment to the welfare of the local community as evidenced by positions of responsibility in community organizations and/or personal contributions to community improvement.

Description: The community board's responsibilities include the following:

To make policy governing the conduct of a PASS Community Free School (i.e., employment, financial planning, educational goals and objectives, fund-raising, etc.).

To participate in raising the necessary funds to support a Community Free School.
To develop sound fiscal policies and oversee the implementation of these policies. To further an understanding of the goals and objectives of the PASS Model within the local community.

PROGRAM DIRECTOR

Qualifications:

1. A graduate degree and/or equivalent experience in education, demonstrated by permanent certification, significant service within the field and experience in innovative programs.

2. Flexibility in dealing with students, parents and community.

3. The ability to implement and direct innovative programs as demonstrated by prior activities.

4. The ability to operate independently within guidelines established by the community board.

5. The ability to communicate effectively both verbally and through writing (i.e., direct meetings, proposals, etc.), to project a positive image of the PASS Community Free School.

6. The ability to design and develop meaningful and creative evaluation.

Description: The role of the program director of a Community Free School is to implement, with the direction of the principal, policies developed by the community board. The program director is responsible for the daily operations of the Community Free School including:

1. Program Development
2. Program Evaluation
3. Inside and Outside Course Programs.

EDUCATIONAL CONSULTANT

Responsibilities: The major responsibility of the educational consultant is to advise the board of education and the community board in matters concerning the implementation of the educational model which is the basis of the PASS Community Free School. In fulfilling this responsibility it is expected that the educational consultant will consult with the district superintendent, the principal of the high school, the community board, the program director, the facilitator, the administrator, the community coordinator, and the teaching staff of a Community Free School. The educational consultant should have full knowledge of and participate in all matters pertaining to the in-school lives and work of teachers, students, and staff.

The educational consultant should be consulted on all appointments to the professional and paraprofessional staff; should consult with the appropriate persons on all curriculum matters before decisions are made; should be informed of all meetings concerning a Community Free School; should be able to visit freely within the houses in order to observe the program in operation and to assist the teachers in planning and improving the learning-teaching situation.

As a secondary responsibility, the educational consultant should be responsible for the conduct of a continuing program of educational research and program evaluation in order to better perform the primary responsibility of this position.

FACILITATOR

Role: In order to implement a new educational program, it is necessary to have someone who is involved on a daily basis in maintaining the innovative aspects of the educational model. Experience has shown that unless such daily implementation is an integral part of the plan, bureaucratic traditions of the public system will eventually displace and eliminate the innovative aspects of the educational model. It is the role of the facilitator, then, to insure that these are implemented and maintained in both the daily and long run operation of a Community Free School. In carrying out this function, the organized responsibilities of the facilitator include the following.

Responsibilities:

1. Organizing meetings to deal with particular aspects of implementation, e.g., family group structure and unity, team teaching;

2. Observation of students and teachers in learning-teaching situations, e.g., classes, conferences, workshops, and labs;

3. Curriculum development, e.g., working with students and teachers in short- and long-range planning and methods;

4. Teacher-training on both a daily and long range basis;

5. Assisting in the development of the outside programs, e.g., working with community coordinator and business advisory board; relating outside programs to programs within each house.

ADMINISTRATOR OR ADMINISTRATIVE ASSISTANT

Role: To act as an expeditor for a Community Free School; to be knowledgeable about the public school system in order to provide materials, supplies, equipment, furniture for a Community Free School; to know procedures for filling out the various forms the school district demands; to make suggestions as to how to work as efficiently as possible within the public school system and still sustain the total educational program.

Responsibilities:

1. Communicate information between the Community Free School and the high school (e.g., college nights, deadlines for filling out forms, etc.);

2. Make teachers aware of the necessary forms to be filled out and how to execute this (e.g., monthly reports, memos, etc.);

3. Obtain furniture and equipment for the Community Free School from the high school or other areas within the system.

4. Requisition new books, materials, supplies, furniture and equipment when necessary;

5. Help teachers obtain textbooks and other learning materials from the high school or other areas from within the system;

6. Inform the Community Free School community regarding the procedures followed at the mother school in areas of discipline, attendance, fire drills, etc.;

7. Assist in maintaining the physical structure of the Community Free School (e.g., making certain the custodian is adequately supplied, that heating is sufficient, etc.).

COMMUNITY COORDINATOR AND OFFICE

Role:

A. Has the responsibility for the outside program:

1. Making contact with outside institutions, organizations and businesses;

2. Making contact with outside instructors;

3. Following up progress, including guidance of learning situation for both teacher and student;

4. Evaluating courses in varied fields of interest.

B. Responsible for recording the attendance of outside courses and passing on this information to family teachers.

C. Explain the philosophy of the Community Free School to community residents, institutions and businesses.

D. Counsel students and teachers about outside courses and post high school training. Act as a resource and counseling center for the family teachers who will counsel their students about post high school aspirations including college training.

E. Has the responsibility to help each house set up an information center and to provide each house with this information.

Qualifications: The community coordinator should:

1. Fully understand the goals and objectives of the PASS Community Free School;

2. Have experience in and ability to deal with executives and managers of business and industry;

3. Be creative and flexible as evidenced by other positions held;

4. Be able to relate well to students and teachers;

5. Have knowledge of experience with learning-teaching theories and methods.

IMPLEMENTATION:

ORGANIZATION AND FLOW OF INFORMATION

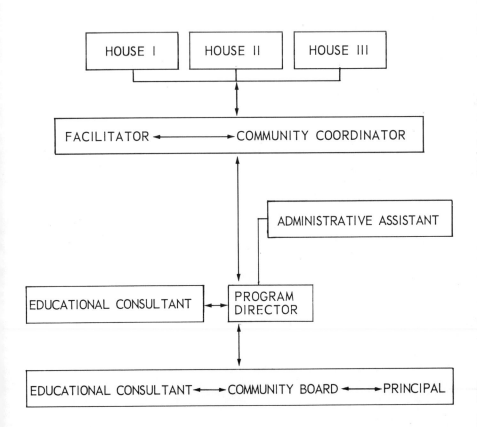

APPENDIX C

COURSE SELECTION GUIDE

Course Number	Course Title		Day/Time		Location	No. of Students
401	Animated Film-making		Tu.	1-3:30	3625 Walnut St.	8-10
402	Arts & Crafts		Th.	1-3:00	4226 Spruce St.	15
403	Communications Arts	Sec. I.	M.	1-3:00	3625 Walnut St.	30
			Th.	9-11:00		
		Sec. II	M.	10-12:00		
			Th.	1-3:00		
404	Techniques of Drawing & Art		W.	2-4:00	Rm. 748, Univ. of Penna. Franklin Bldg.	6
405	Photography		M.	8:30-10:00	3625 Walnut St.	4
406	Dramatic Arts		Tu.	10-11:30	Houston Hall Univ. of Pa.	10
407	Dance Theory & Technique		M. & Tu. 2-4:00		YGS — 33rd & Haverford	12-14
408	Piano, Organ		F.	11-12:30	Phila. Divinity Sch. — 42nd & Locust	1
409	Modern Dance		W.	2-3:30	YGS — 33rd & Haverford	10
410	Art & Awareness		M.	10-12:00		16-18
			W.	1-4:00	3625 Walnut St.	
411	Introduction to Drawing		Th.	10-12:00	4226 Spruce St.	10-12
412	Violin Instructions		Tu. &	3:00		6
			Th.		510 S. 41st St.	
413	Theater Workshop		W.	10-12:00	Irvine Aud. Rm. 35 Univ. of Pa.	12-15
414	Visual Arts Workshop		Tu.	9-11:00	Fine Arts. Bldg.	8-10
			Th.		Univ. of Pa.	
415	Writing Workshop		Tu.	1-2:30	3625 Walnut St.	10-15
			Th.			
451	Introduction to African Culture		W.	9:30-11:00	3914 Locust St.	10
			Th.			
452	Library Science		M.	1-4:00	Veterans Admin. Hospital	1
			W.			
453	Islamic Civilization		Tu.	10-11:30	Van Pelt Library Univ. of Pa.	5-10
454	Racism		Tu.	1-3:00	Phil. Divinity School 42nd & Spruce	8

Appendix C

Course Number	Course Title		Day/Time		Location	No. of Students
455	Public Relations in Public T.V.		Tu. Th.	2-4:00	4548 Market St.	5-6
456	History in the Making		W.	1-3:00	Phil Divinity School 42nd & Spruce	8
457	Our Dirty Philadelphia	Sec. I	W. F.	9-10:30 1-3:00	3625 Walnut St.	8
		Sec. II	Th. F.	10-11:30 1-3:00		
458	Modern Day Ethics		F. Tu. & Th.	1-3:00 1-2:00	University of Pa.	10-12
459	History of Western Culture		W.	1-3:00	Phila. Divinity School 42nd & Spruce	8
460	India & Modern World		F.	10-12:00	Logan Hall Univ. of Pa.	5-10
461	The Law		Tu. Th.	4-5:00 10-3:00	3625 Walnut St.	10-12
462	Ethical Values in African Culture		Th.	10:30-12:00	3740 Spruce St. Newman Hall	25
463	Pocket Park		W.	10-12:00	3625 Walnut St.	10
464	Housing & Welfare Rights		Th.	1-3:00	4410 Fairmount	4
465	Community Newsletter		M. W.	1-3:00 2-3:00	3603 Hamilton St.	3-5
466	How to Poll Public Opinion		Tu. & Th.	2:30-3:30	Chestnut between 56th & 57th	6
467	Early Childhood Study		M. & W.	1:30-3:30	Elementary Schools	28
468	Patient Rehabilitation		M.	1-3:00	Children's Hosp. 1740 Bainbridge	2
469	The Role of the Church in a Community				59th St. Baptist Church	30
501	Pharmacy Lab		M. W.	9-12:00	Veterans Admin. Hospital	1
502	Drafting Techniques		W.	2-4:00	Rm. 748, Franklin Bldg.	6
503	Astronomy		Th.	3:30-5:00	4N6 Rittenhouse Lab. U. of Pa.	10
504	Bio-Chemistry Research				Univ. of Penn.	7

156

Course Number	Course Title	Day/Time	Location	No. of Students
505	Topics in Animal Biology	Tu. 10-11:30	Rm. 151-152-School of Veterinary Med.	12-15
506	Brain Power	W. 2-3:30	Rm. 243 Anatomy-Chem. Bldg. U.of P.	2-3
507	Basic Electrical Theory	M. 2-3:00 F.	51 N. 39th St.	1
508	Physics	W. 10-12:00	Rm. 1N10 Rittenhouse Lab. U. of P.	2
509	Basic Concepts of Math	Tu. 11-12:00 W. 10-11:00	Moore Sch. 33rd. & Walnut St.	10
510	Math & Computer Programming Sec. 1 / Sec. II.	Tu. & Th. 1:30-2:30 W. 2:30-3:30 M. Tu. & Th. 2:30-3:30	House II & III	30+
511	Anesthesiology	M. 1-3:00	Children's Hosp.	2
512	Home Economics	F. 9-11:00	Phila. Gas Works 5230 Chestnut	17
551	Clerical Training & Practice	Th. 2-4:00	Fidelity Bank Broad & Chestnut	1
552	Radio Broadcasting	W. 10-3:00	WIBG Radio 117 Ridge Pike	3-5
553	Financing & Newspaper	M. & W. 3-4:30	Daily Pennsylvanian - U. of Pa.	3
554	The World of Construction	Tu. W. Th. 2-5:00	Sites Construction	8
555	Ham Radio Operation	Th. & F. 1-2:00	Moore School of Engineering	15
556	Orientation to Life Insurance	Th. 9:30-11:30	46th & Market	6
557	Communication-Public Relations	M. 1-3:00	College Hall Univ. of Pa.	5-6
558	Magazine Publishing	Th. 2-4:00	Am. College of Physicians-4200 Pine St.	2-3
559	Fundamentals of TV Production	M. 10-12:00	WPHL-TV Channel 17	10
560	Training of a Machinist	M. & F. 2-3:00	51 N. 39th St.	1
561	Dietetics & Food Prep.	Tu. & F. 9-12:00	Veterans Adm. Hosp.	2

Appendix C

Course Number	Course Title	Day/Time		Location	No. of Students
562	Office Practice in Med. Admin.	Sec. I.	M. & Th. 1-4:00		
		Sec. II.	Tu. & F. 1-4:00	Veterans Adm. Hosp.	4
563	Intro. to Dentistry	Sec. I.	M. 9:30-11:30		
		Sec. II.	Th. 9:00-12:00	U. of Pa. Dental	
		Sec. III.	Th. 2:00-5:00	School	30
564	Office Training & Practice		M. & W. 1-4:00	Vet. Admin. Hospital	3
565	Nursing		Tu. 9-12:00 W. 1-4:00	Phila. Gen. Hosp.	8
566	Clerical Practice		Tu. & Th. 1-4:00	Veterans Adm. Hosp.	1
567	Library & Office Practice		M. & W. 9-12:00	Veterans Adm. Hosp.	3
568	Social Work		T. & W. 1-4:00	Veterans Adm. Hosp.	4
569	Stenography & Typing		Tu. & Th. 3-4:30	431 N. 39th St.	14
570	Clerical Training		M. 2-4:00	Fidelity Bank	1
571	Clerical Practice		Tu. 2-4:00	Fidelity Bank	1
572	Clerical Training		F. 3-5:00	Fidelity Bank	1
573	Data Processing		Tu. 2-4:00	Franklin Bldg.	2
574	Office Training		W. 3-5:00	Fidelity Bank	1
575	Functions of a Commercial Bank		W. 2-4:00	Fidelity Bank 2401 Penna. Ave.	15
576	Paving			Phila Gas Works	2
577	Bank Operations		W. 1-4:00	Girard Trust Bank Broad & Chestnut	4
578	Personal Money Management		W. 10-11:00	First Penna Co. 3020 Market St.	15
579	Basic Electricity		F. 9-11:00	Phila Gas Works	17
579a	Vehicle Repairs			Phila Gas Works	2
580	Printing			Chilton Co. Chestnut between 56th & 57th	3
581	Post Office Operation		F. 9:30-11:30	Rm 574 US Post Office 30th & Market	8

Course Number	Course Title	Day/Time	Location	No. of Students
582	Public Relations	M. 1-3:00	Children's Hosp.	1
583	Display Advertising		Phila Gas Works	2
584	Telephone Answering		Phila Gas Works	2
585	General Office Training		Phila Gas Works	20
586	Newspaper Photography	M. - W. 2-4:00	Daily Penna	2
587	Newspaper Reporting	T. & Th. 2:30-4:00	Daily Penna	3
588	Engineering		Phila Gas Works	2
589	Research & Development		Phila Gas Works	2
590	Finance & Accounting		Phila Gas Works	2

COURSE TITLES

Animated Film-making
Arts & Crafts
Communication Arts
Techniques of Drawing & Art
Photography
Dramatic Arts
Dance Theory & Technique
Piano, Organ
Modern Dance
Art & Awareness
Introduction to Drawing
Violin Instructions
Theater Workshop
Visual Arts Workshop
Writing Workshop
Introduction to African Culture
Library Science
Islamic Civilization
Racism
Public Relations in Public T.V.
History in the Making
Our Dirty Philadelphia
Modern Day Ethics
History of Western Culture
India & Modern World

Housing & Welfare Rights
Community Newsletter
How to Poll Public Opinion
Early Childhood Study
Patient Rehabilitation
The Role of the Church in a Community
Pharmacy Lab
Drafting Techniques
Astronomy
Bio-Chemistry Research
Topics in Animal Biology
Brain Power
Basic Electrical Theory
Physics
Basic Concepts of Math
Math & Computer Programming
Anesthesiology
Home Economics
Clerical Training & Practice
Radio Broadcasting
Financing & Newspaper
The World of Construction
Ham Radio Operation
Orientation to Life Insurance
Communication-Public Relations

Appendix C

The Law
Ethical Values in African Culture
Pocket Park
Dietetics & Food Prep.
Office Practice in Med. Admin.
Intro. to Dentistry
Office Training & Practice
Nursing
Clerical Practice
Library & Office Practice
Social Work
Stenography & Typing
Clerical Training
Clerical Practice
Data Processing
Office Training
Functions of a Commercial Bank
Paving
Bank Operations

Magazine Publishing
Fundamentals of TV Production
Training of a Machinist
Personal Money Management
Basic Electricity
Printing
Post Office Operation
Public Relations
Display Advertising
Telephone Answering
General Office Training
Newspaper Photography
Newspaper Reporting
Engineering
Research & Development
Finance & Accounting
Vehicle Repairs

REFERENCES

PUBLICATIONS RELATED TO THE WEST PHILADELPHIA
COMMUNITY FREE SCHOOL PROJECT

Aase Eriksen	– *Scattered Schools* Report to HEW from Planning Grant 1970-71 Second printing made possible by grant from Educational Facilities Laboratories.
Aase Eriksen and Judith Messina	– "The Dynamics of Leadership in an Informal School" *Journal of Research and Development in Education* Vol. 5, No. 3, Spring 1972
Aase Eriksen and Joseph Gantz	– "Business in Public Education" *Wharton Quarterly*, Summer 1971
Aase Eriksen and Judith Messina	– "Community Involvement: Scattered Schools, An Urban Experiment" *Urban and Social Change Review*, December 1972
Aase Eriksen and Frederick Fiske	– "Teacher Adaptation to an Informal School" *NASSP Bulletin*, January 1973
Frederick Fiske	– "The Free School: A Self-portrait"
Lester Velie	– "Give Us This Day Our ABC's" *Readers Digest*, December 1971
Nancy Schniederwind	– "The Community Free School" *Strawberry Statement*, James S. Kunen Avon Publication, 1970

Curriculum materials prepared under the direction of Aase Eriksen with grants from:

The W. Clement and Jessie V. Stone Foundation teacher/writer, Frederick Fiske:

"The American Dream" – A social studies unit.

The Samuel S. Fels Foundation, teachers/writers, Jolly Bruce, Michael Brown, Joseph Gantz, Hannah Goldfarb, Art Hyde, Steven Marcus, Lynne Miller, Anne Sattler, Nancy Schniederwind, Elaine Simon, Gary Watts, Sidney Zilber.

Units:

Election Simulation
Psychology: Freudian Theory
Immigration
Protest, Politics, and Change
Using Music to Teach the Humanities
Ways of Knowing Yourself

INDEX

Index

Index

1961